Happy Birthday!

love from Simon and

Becky

X

DISCOVERING ESSEX IN LONDON

You lived here!

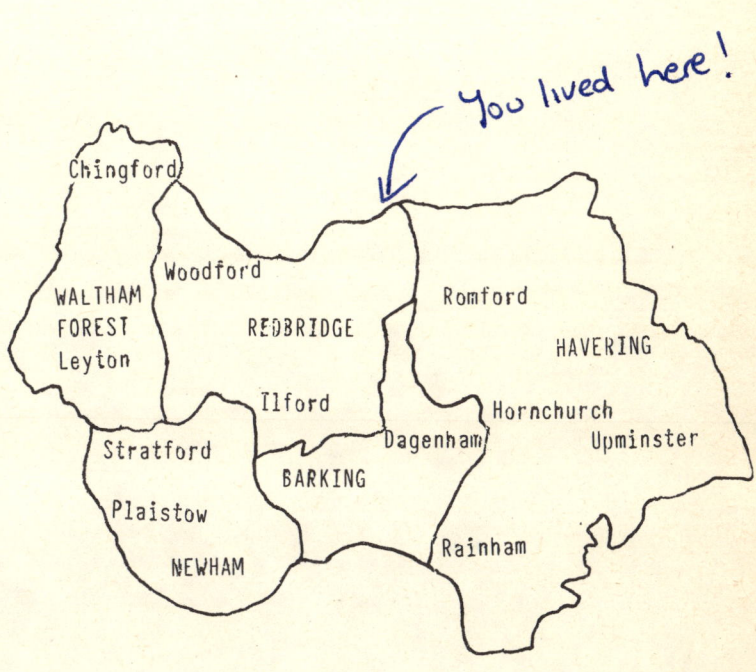

The smock mill of Upminster

DISCOVERING
ESSEX
IN LONDON

by
Kenneth Neale

IAN HENRY PUBLICATIONS

First published by
Essex Countryside, 1969
This edition, 1986

ISBN 0 86025 406 2

The cover photograph is of
Pimp Hall Farm, Chingford
about 1965
Photograph by C O Harvey

Printed in Great Britain by WBC Print Ltd, Bristol

CONTENTS

The Old Rectory, Woodford

PREFACE

IT is commonly accepted that books, particularly those with a philosophical or historical flavour, are written with a view to influencing the minds of those who the author hopes will read them. To the extent that the interpretation of any theme exposes the reader to the opinions of the writer this is true of this book also. But that is not its purpose. I have been impressed during the last few years with the strength of the feeling of belonging to Essex rather than London which still persists in the boroughs to the east of the Lea. It is only realistic, however, to expect that in the course of time the allegiance of Greater Londoners to the Home Counties will be eroded. Who in Hackney or Islington now regard themselves as the inheritors of a Middlesex tradition? I believe nevertheless that geographical and sociological factors will tend to prolong the process of assimilation in metropolitan Essex. I have composed this book, therefore, in the hope that it will prove of interest to the general reader, of use to students and of value to those who cherish their affinities with the county as well as with the capital; and because it seemed worth while.

Except in the organization and presentation of its theme and the limited use I have made of the products of my own research into Essex history the book has no claim to originality. In common with most writers in the historical and topographical fields, I am indebted to numerous predecessors, some of whose works I have included in the reference note. I am grateful also to the editor of *Essex Countryside*, who has kindly allowed me to draw to some extent on the articles I have contributed to the county magazine over the past few years. Where I have done so the text has been largely rewritten. I have had, too, the benefit of recent research by Mr. W. H. Liddell, of the University of London, who kindly read the forest chapter and offered many helpful suggestions. It remains only to add that anyone working on the history of the new boroughs will necessarily avail himself, as I have, of the *Victoria County History* and the excellent services and publications of the Essex Record Office.   KENNETH NEALE.

Chingford.
January 1969.

Valence House, Dagenham

PREFACE
(reprint of 1986)

READERS of this reprinted edition of *Discovering Essex in London* will see that in the 1969 preface I remarked upon the persistent strength of the Essex tradition in the London boroughs. Judging by the devotion of the local historical societies to the county and its history that is still true. However, change is continuous. Since the book was written the processes of topographical and administrative change and recent economic problems have made their impact. The most conspicuous of these changes have been urban and residential re-development, the construction of the motorways, the massive run-down and re-habilitation of dockland and the recent abolition of the Greater London Council. For historians there has been the accumulation of new knowledge through research and discovery such as the latest evaluation of the Roman site of Durolitum. Nevertheless, the text of the book, even allowing for these changes, remains, in its historical and descriptive aspects, a valid interpretation of the metropolitan areas of the traditional county.

Certainly the spirit of Essex remains as part of the idiom of life in the area which owes its heritage to the county and for which the county still provides a rural and recreational dimension. In these terms the changes, though significant in some places, have not been dramatic in their overall effect. That particular drama was a phenomenon of the nineteenth century which has been re-defined and endorsed by recent events.

I would like to think that the book still offers an encouraging stimulus to the interest and enjoyment of these Essex traditions and the richness inherent in the life and history of the boroughs. I am grateful, therefore, that Ian Henry Publications have decided to reprint this book, long out-of-print, albeit in the original text, and for their helpful and positive cooperation in that.

KENNETH NEALE

Great Sampford, 1986.

The Spotted Dog

FOREWORD

THE original kingdom of Essex embraced a large area which it lost not long afterwards. This became Middlesex and included London, its capital. It took well over 1,000 years of London's growth to reverse the process. Eventually, in 1965, London appropriated the whole of Middlesex and at the same time a large part of Essex was ceded to become " Essex in London." But more than 1,000 years of history leave a multitude of marks. The spirit of this part of the ancient county endures, and this book symbolizes the strength of the spirit.

Kenneth Neale is well known to thousands of readers of his " Essex in London " feature in *Essex Countryside*, a monthly reminder of the historical background of current developments. He has done a great deal more as chairman of the lively Chingford Historical Society, which recently gave me the signal honour of its presidency in succession to Sir Winston Churchill. He now covers his wide field in detail which is so absorbing that a first reading will be followed, I feel sure, by second and third readings, and then by frequent reference to individual chapters. This indeed has been my own reaction, as a fortunate reader in advance of others. I have already learned so much that is fresh about this part of Essex that I thought I knew. The secret of Kenneth Neale's remarkable book lies in his living here and looking at it with double vision so that he sees those interlacing strands of history which together make up a unique product, " Essex in London and London in Essex."

Almost every page has a surprising bit for the reader, telling him of the Roman cemetery discovered at Temple Mills, Leyton, in the seventeenth century; of the finding in 1911 of the elaborately ornamented shaft of a Saxon cross built into the wall of Barking parish church; of the way in which many watermills in West Ham marked in 1777 on the great Essex map of Chapman and André can be traced back to eight in the Domesday Book; of the annual fair held on Havering green for over three centuries from 1465; of the charcoal-burners (coal-yers) working in the depths of the forest who gave their name to Collier Row; of the 1,400 fishermen who manned the great Barking " Short Blue " Hewitt fleet as late as 1850; of the experiments around 1700 of the clerical scientists William Derham of Upminster, who used his church tower as an observatory, and James Pound of Wanstead, who set up the world's largest telescope in the park; of the history of the little " red bridge " which was to give its name in 1965 to the great borough.

Use Kenneth Neale's book as a guide to discovering fresh places of interest.

F. G. EMMISON,
County archivist of Essex.

Chelmsford.
February 1969.

The stocks on Havering Green

Chapter 1

INTRODUCING ESSEX IN LONDON

WITHIN the quadrant formed by the Thames and the Lea, the ancient river boundaries of the county, lies Essex in London. It is a major urban concentration of industry and dormitory suburbs and an area of striking contrasts. In the eastern reaches, beyond the Ingrebourne river, are the arable farmlands of Havering, which blend imperceptibly into Essex. To the north, in Redbridge and Waltham Forest, the suburban scene is enriched by the lakes, woods and glades of Epping Forest. But the southern horizons are dominated by the masts and cranes of Newham's dockland and the giant installations of industrial Thames-side at Barking. Only along the forest periphery and in the rural margins of Havering can we readily recall the Essex countryside as it was before London overflowed.

Lying within the shadow of the metropolis, it was for more than 1,000 years an integral part of Essex, and its origins are deeply embedded in the life and history of the county. The pervading influence of the capital has never been absent from the life of the area, and its future is tied immutably to that of London. But the links between Essex and London, political, social and economic, have been numerous and strong. The vicissitudes of the capital have invariably had repercussions in the county; their interests have usually coincided. The new Greater London boroughs thus share a common heritage, the sources of which spring from the rich seams of the historical and cultural traditions of London as well as of rural Essex.

It was not until the middle of the nineteenth century that London began, decisively, to encroach on the Home Counties. From about this time various social and economic factors combined to promote the growth of industry beyond the London boundaries, and this development spread eastwards over the Lea into the low-lying marshlands and meadows of the south-west corner of Essex. Simultaneously railways and roads were constructed to supplement the traditional river lines of communication and the population of the area began to increase rapidly. Later, towards the end of the century, the process of urbanization extended northwards into what is now Waltham Forest and Redbridge. It was halted only on the boundary of Epping Forest, made inviolate by the Act of 1878.

The phenomenal economic and social development of the area led inevitably to changes in the structure of local government which culminated in the Local Government Act of 1963. Under this Act large and important parts of Essex, Surrey, Hertfordshire and Kent, and three county boroughs, including East and West Ham, were incorporated in Greater London. Middlesex was wholly consumed. Although only about six per cent of the land area of Essex was transferred more than half its population and rateable value was involved. What had been London in Essex became, in April 1965, Essex in London.

King George V Dock

Chapter 2

THE HISTORICAL BACKGROUND

1. Emergent Essex

THE period of recorded history and even of our archæological knowledge is but a moment of time in the infinite past that recedes far into the geological ages and beyond. The flat, gaunt acres of the Thames-side levels and the undulating woodlands of the forest boroughs are but the subdued residue of geological and climatic cycles measured not in centuries, or even in millenniums, but in millions of years. Almost beyond the frontiers of imagination the whole area evolved as part of a continent of drenching tropical rain forests and great torrential rivers. These epochs were succeeded by the recurring arctic conditions of the Ice Ages and eventually by milder climates and an environment in which human life could be sustained. But long before then the remote ancestors of contemporary beasts, creatures long extinct, possessed the territory that climatic changes and human ingenuity delivered into the hands of man.

The chalk and clay foundations of south-west Essex, which forms part of the London basin, have yielded ample evidence of the prehistoric animal life of the area. Since early in the nineteenth century relics of this primeval past have been recovered during excavations along the river valleys. Embedded in the glacial debris and in the gravel terraces formed during interglacial periods by the falling levels of the Thames and the Lea, then rivers of mighty proportions, have been found the fossilized remains of woolly rhinoceros, mammoth, bison, elk and reindeer, as well as molluscs and other vestiges of marine life. Perhaps the most remarkable find was that of the skull and tusks, over eight feet in length, of a mammoth unearthed at Uphall, Ilford, and now in the British Museum. Similar if less spectacular discoveries have been made along the course of the Roding, in the glacier-borne rocks at Hornchurch and in the Thames-side gravels at Rainham. In the Lea valley the excavation of the reservoirs and the construction of the navigation channels exposed further relics of the same forms of prehistoric life. Here and there throughout the whole area, on the arc from Pole Hill at Chingford to Rainham down by the Thames, there is geological evidence of the extremities of the glaciation which extended southwards to roughly the line of the Thames Valley.

When man enters our story we must think in terms of scattered primitive communities dominated by their environment. Technically they were unable to cope with the problems posed by the difficult clay soils and the heavily wooded terrain. There was no settled agriculture or methodic cultivation even in a rudimentary form. These prehistoric people were mainly nomadic tribesmen subsisting on the fruits of their hunting in the forest, or riverine dwellers relying on the rivers for their sustenance and communications. We know little about the earliest inhabitants of the area, but the Roman annals and the results of archæological research have enabled historians to piece together a broadly coherent picture of the Celtic tribes that occupied the Lea valley and the lands eastwards to the sea in the periods before the Roman invasions. By that time these immigrant peoples—for they originated from continental Europe—had settled themselves on the land, which they farmed on a simple but systematic basis. There were also viable elements of political organization and established commercial and cultural relationships with Gaul and the Low Countries. It was these people who confronted and were overwhelmed by the military prowess of the legions and subjected to the ordered supremacy of Rome.

The most familiar date in English history is 1066, and after that comes 55 B.C.; but in fact Julius Cæsar's foray into Britain in that year was little more than a probe. The Cæsarian invasion of the following year was motivated by more serious objectives. The Romans then carried their military thrusts into Hertfordshire and the Lea valley before withdrawing when the enterprise was undermined by a serious revolt among the indigenous tribes in Gaul, ethnically akin to Cæsar's victims in Britain, and by mounting political dissension in Rome itself. But Roman interest had been so stimulated by the two expeditions that the influence of the empire in Britain, commercial and cultural, continued to increase. Thus was the way prepared for the success of the Claudian invasion of A.D. 43, when Aulus Plautius, commanding a force of some

50,000 men, defeated the Britons in Kent. Plautius next forced the Medway and negotiated the Thames. Essex, which the Romans were to develop as an area of considerable strategic importance, lay at the mercy of the Roman army. Striking across the tactically indefensible heart of Essex, the legions, with Claudius himself now at their head, reduced Camulodunum (Colchester), the tribal capital, and received the submission of the Trinovantes. The inhabitants of south-west Essex thus first experienced the firm clasp of strong government and came within the ambit of an authority based initially on Colchester but within two decades on London (Londinium), which the Romans developed as the capital of the newly won province. From this time may be dated the beginning of the process that after almost 2,000 years culminated in the Greater London of today.

Although the site of London had been occupied before the Romans they were the first to recognize and exploit its economic and strategic potential. It thus became the principal Roman settlement and the focus of the impressive system of road communications that radiated from it. Northwards from London, roughly parallel with the west bank of the Lea, ran Ermine Street. Eastwards the great military road to the Roman colonia at Colchester traversed the Lea and the marshlands at Old Ford, a causeway being constructed of herringbone paving. From the causeway the route went via Ilford, Romford and Chelmsford. A subordinate route, passing through Chigwell, connected at Great Dunmow with Stane Street, which itself provided an east-west link between Ermine Street and Colchester. It is not clear whether this secondary road forked from the main route to the colonia or entered London at another point. The London—Colchester road provided the strategic axis from which the Romans dominated Essex, which thus came under imperial rule from the outset although nearly a century was to elapse before the remainder of Britain, apart from Scottish highland areas, was subjugated.

One of the most dramatic episodes during almost four centuries of Roman rule in Britain occurred soon after the Claudian occupation when, in A.D. 61, the Iceni, under their chieftainess Boadicea, provoked beyond endurance by their Roman rulers, revolted. Joined by some dissident elements of the Trinovantes, the rampaging and vengeful tribal host savagely destroyed the principal Roman centres in the south-east at Colchester, London and St. Albans with fearful loss of life. Until the final disintegration of Roman authority in the island province the Iceni rising posed the most serious threat to their security that the Roman commanders had to endure. Their position in East Anglia, Essex and London was virtually destroyed by the merciless assaults on their strongholds. Recoiling under the weight and ferocity of the insurrection, the Romans were in a precarious situation. The Ninth Hispana legion was almost annihilated, only the cavalry formations surviving. This desperate situation was not restored until Suetonius Paulinus, with a strong force drawn from the Fourteenth Gemina and Twentieth Valeria Victrix legions, and auxiliary troops summoned from Anglesey, where they were campaigning, brought Boadicea's followers to battle. The tactical superiority, experience and discipline of the Roman veterans prevailed and the tribal army was decisively defeated. Boadicea fled from the scene of the encounter to her death. Local tradition asserts that the dramatic counter blow by Suetonius occurred at Ambresbury Banks in Epping Forest and the poignant scene in which Boadicea is said to have poisoned herself is placed at Cobbins Brook, beyond Copt Hall, just south-west of Epping, but there is no historical evidence for this and the actual battleground remains unknown.

In what is now the Greater London area of Essex there were a number of minor Roman settlements. Fairly extensive Roman remains were discovered in the early eighteenth century during work on the Leyton Grange estate, some of the items finding their way into the private collection of the local vicar, John Strype, whom we shall meet elsewhere in this book. The foundations of Roman buildings were seen to extend over some two acres and included a Roman pavement and the remains of arched doorways with associated pottery and coins. Elsewhere in Leyton, at Ruckholts and at Temple Mills, burial urns and sarcophagi indicating the site of a Roman cemetery were unearthed by gravel diggers in the seventeenth century. At a somewhat greater distance from the military road, at Walthamstow, there is as yet no evidence of a Roman occupation site, but there and to a lesser extent at Chingford an abundance of coins, pottery, tools and weapons has been recovered from the Lea valley. At Wanstead a Romano-British villa or farm settlement was exposed and a tessellated pavement, unfortunately destroyed during building operations about 150 years ago, on the site of the great house now Wanstead Park. The surrounding area continues, from time to time, to yield fragments of Roman tiles and pottery. Still awaiting archæological proof is Stukeley's theory that Romford was once the site of a Roman military post. On the military road between London and Colchester there are known to have been three military stations. One was at Cæsaromagus (Chelmsford) and another at Canonium (probably Rivenhall), where there is evidence of a Roman settlement. The third, Durolitum, was probably at Gidea Park, but beyond a few isolated and inconclusive documentary references there is no evidence with which to substantiate this location, though the Romford area is on the Roman route which passes through the market place. It is also at about the right interval, since, as with the siting of the other two intermediate stations, Durolitum was said to be roughly equidistant between Londinium and Cæsaromagus.

Although therefore there is ample evidence of the integration of the area into the Roman province it was never developed on any scale. To the extent that the Romans did exploit the area this largely reflected its proximity to London and the main lines of communication with Roman Colchester. And so it was throughout subsequent history: never beyond the influence of the capital; always essentially within the life of the county. But the real foundations of the modern communities of Essex in London were laid in the Anglo-Saxon period between the end of Roman rule and the advent of the Normans.

The course of events in the fifth and sixth centuries is often obscure, and we do not know with any precision the chronology and manner of the Anglo-Saxon occupation. As we have seen, the whole edifice of Roman authority had been shaken to the roots in A.D. 61, but reserves had been available and the empire was still in the ascendancy. This was not so at the beginning of the fifth century. Under the stress of external pressure and internal disruption the physical and moral resources of Rome were consumed. Morale was eroded as the provinces in northern Europe disintegrated. The Roman abdication in Britain became inevitable. Britain, already infiltrated by peaceful settlement, was ripe for the next phase of the long recurrent invasions by continental adventurers. Rome itself was sacked by Alaric's barbarian hordes in A.D. 410.

★　★　★　★

As the Roman empire crumbled the movement across Europe of the heathen tribesmen was intensified. The western movement into

Britain, ultimately decisive in historical terms, was concentrated on the coasts and the river routes of eastern and southern Britain. The Saxons first possessed themselves of the land we now call Sussex. They also settled in Essex and other areas in the south. The Angles established themselves in what has come to be known as East Anglia. The Jutes colonized Kent. This is a gross over-simplification of the patterns of settlement, but it conveys the broad picture and for convenience we refer to these disparate tribal groupings as the Anglo-Saxons. In Essex settlement along the Thames, the Lea, the Colne and the Chelmer was fairly well established by the end of the sixth century. The process is uncertain, but by then the East Saxon kingdom had developed. From the beginning its political links were with the Jutes in Kent rather than with the Angles to the north. Possibly that anomalous part of Kent on the Essex bank of the Thames at North Woolwich, which persisted until 1965, when it was combined in Newham, had its origins in this association. Further evidence of the connection is provided by the Jutish cemeteries which have been excavated at Rainham, where also was recovered a magnificent glass drinking horn of Saxon origin. When the kingdom of Essex did expand its sphere of influence it was to the west to include Middlesex, parts of Hertfordshire and, of special relevance to this study, London. But the East Saxon kings, with their oddly alliterative names, were usually subordinate in a degree to more powerful kings in Kent, Mercia or Wessex who enjoyed their allegiance. Essex as a political entity never seems to have been wholly free from the influence of the paramount Anglo-Saxon kingdoms. Thus it was that Aethelbert of Kent prevailed upon his nephew, Sebert of Essex, to accept the Christian faith at the beginning of the seventh century. In A.D. 665 Sigebert was in turn persuaded by Oswiu, the Northumbrian king, who at the time exercised suzerainty over Kent and Essex, to accept the Celtic bishop Cedd. During the heptarchy Essex was subordinated to Mercia and by the ninth century to Egbert of Wessex.

The fate of London after the Roman withdrawal has for a long time puzzled and intrigued historians. The theory that the site was abandoned no longer holds, as archæological investigation has revealed sufficient evidence to show that a Romano-British population lingered in the decaying town. Organized life appears to have continued, albeit at a very low level, and London was never entirely deserted. Its revival in due course was inevitable because of the basic advantages of its geographical situation. The invaders settled in all the adjacent areas, but there is little evidence of early Saxon settlement within the old walled city itself. The Saxons were primarily a farming people and tended to establish themselves on productive land, and were not attracted to town life. But by the end of the seventh century London had grown in importance as a trading centre, many of its commercial links being with the old homelands of the Saxon colonists. Some of the settlements in southwest Essex date from the early stages of the Anglo-Saxon occupation, as is evidenced by the place-names ending in " ing," " ton " and " ham," such as Barking, Havering, Wennington, Leyton and the Hams. Others in the more difficult terrain on the forest ridge, such as Wanstead, Woodford and Chingford, were later. It was not until the Saxons colonized the area that a cohesive and well-organized society was developed in this part of Essex.

It is a remarkable fact that these heathen and rugged fighting folk possessed innate political wisdom. Their capacity for creating effective political and social systems is apparent in the continued survival of the institutions which they established. Much of the legal and political apparatus by which we are governed today has its provenance in the Anglo-Saxon kingdoms. The complex and highly developed administrative organization of the Greater London area has evolved from the relatively simple though comprehensive system of the later Anglo-Saxon period. It was at that time that the hundred as a basic unit of local administration first developed in those areas that were not subject to strong Danish influence. Essex was divided into twenty such units. The present Greater London area of Essex broadly comprised the hundred of Becontree, most of the Chafford hundred, the southern part of the Waltham hundred and, later, the Havering liberty. The exact significance of the term " hundred " presents some difficulty and there is no certainty about its interpretation. On the one hand it has been taken as indicating, in its original sense, the grouping for fiscal, political and jurisdictional purposes of 100 families. On the other hand, and more probably, it may always have had geographical significance, as it certainly had at a later stage. Thus it might have constituted the area occupied by 100 families or, alternatively, an area of 100 hides. But the hide does not permit of an exact interpretation, although it is usually taken as being 120 acres. Frequently, however, especially in the southern shires, the hundredal divisions do not correspond to such meaurements. Similarly we cannot be clear about the half-hundred, which term was applied to the Waltham hundred from about the twelfth century, although it appears to have had some practical significance in relation to representation in the itinerant courts. Chingford fell within the Waltham hundred, but most of the area including Walthamstow, Leyton, Redbridge, Newham and Barking comprised the Becontree hundred. The Havering liberty was part of this hundred until 1465. The remainder of present-day Havering was included within the Chafford hundred with South Ockendon and Stifford, which are still in Essex.

Barking abbey, probably founded in A.D. 666, was the principal manorial authority in the Becontree hundred, although both Waltham abbey and the abbey of Stratford Langthorne held land within it. Of the three Barking was the most powerful, its Benedictine influences doing much to offset the Celtic practices deriving from Cedd's foundations at Tilbury and Ithancester (Bradwell-juxta-Mare). The astringent Cistercians at Stratford were more content to devote their energies to their narrower monastic interests, although both of these religious houses played a significant part in the economic development of the area. Christianity first reached Essex in an organized sense following the appointment by Augustine of a bishop, Mellitus, to London with the task of converting the heathen East Saxon kingdom to the Roman faith. He had some initial success, but the task was beyond his slender resources. In A.D. 616 he was reluctantly forced to abandon his mission and the forces of paganism reasserted themselves in the East Saxon kingdom. Thus it was left to the Northumbrian St. Cedd in A.D. 653 to lay the permanent foundations on which the Christian Church in Essex was built. But the prestige and authority of the abbey at Barking grew rapidly after its foundation in A.D. 666. Its secular influence was enhanced by the grant by royal charter of extensive lands in London, Kent and Surrey as well as in Essex. Some indication of the impetus of the abbey's waxing authority may be gauged from the occasion of the death at Barking of Eorcenwald, its founder and fourth bishop to the East Saxons, in April 693. Less than thirty years from the foundation of the abbey Eorcenwald's remains were carried across the Thames-side marshes to London for burial at St. Paul's. A spectacular procession, escorted by torchbearers and mourning monks and nuns, passed through what had not long before been pagan territory. That much is history. Legend tells of miraculous partings of the waters before the cortège at the Roding and the Lea, both of these rivers being in flood as the result of a tumultuous storm.

By the end of the eighth century Saxon England came under pressure from the plundering Scandinavian adventurers whom we call the Vikings. In its earliest phase the Viking marauders contented themselves with sporadic raids during which they would descend without warning on Christian establishments or Saxon homesteads in search of plunder, which they carried back to their northern homes. Barking abbey is believed to have been sacked during one of these raids, which no doubt struck terror into local hearts. But the communities of the London area must have been heartened by the stalwart defence of the town against the Vikings when in A.D. 994 Olaf Tryggvason, with a force of almost 100 ships, was repulsed at London Bridge. Eventually the momentum of the Viking campaigns, which took them to the Danube and across the Atlantic, led to the major expeditions during which they established themselves territorially in Northumbria, Mercia, Wessex and eastern England. The fortunes of the struggle swayed, but the cohesion and ferocity of the Danish assaults, which gave them a tactical superiority, drove the ill-organized and irregular Saxon forces westwards. Essex fell to the invaders in the ninth century and Alfred the Great was forced into a desperate defensive posture, faced with the task of restoring English morale and rebuilding his military forces for the resumed struggle against the strongly ensconced Danes.

Thus it was that Somerset became the heartland of the beleaguered Saxon royal house when much of the country, including Essex, had been subjugated by the invaders. It was from the broad green marshlands of Athelney that the Saxon resurgence which carried the frontiers of Alfredian Wessex to the borders of Essex was launched. After a series of bravely and skilfully conducted engagements the greatest of English kings brought his opponents to the peace table. A small village in the Vale of Avalon gave its name to the so-called Peace of Wedmore, which, following Alfred's victory over Guthrum at Aethandune in 878, " saved England for Christendom " and settled the division of the country between Saxons and Danes. The boundary was fixed along the line of Watling Street and the Thames, and although seven years later Alfred was able to advance his frontiers to the Lea it was Wedmore that confirmed

Essex within the Danelaw under Guthrum. Thereafter there was no question of Alfred recovering the former East Saxon kingdom. That task fell to his son, Edward the Elder, who in a sustained campaign between 911 and 916 drove the Danish forces from Essex. During the reign of Aethelred the Danes once more gained the ascendancy, and following the death of Edmund Ironside, with whom he had shared sovereignty over England, Canute became king of England. However, Danish settlement had never sunk deep roots in Essex, which remained ethnically and culturally Saxon in character, so there was doubtless much rejoicing in Essex when the Saxon royal line was re-established at the accession of Edward the Confessor.

It is perhaps apposite here to digress from history into the realm of legend. Nor is it wholly inappropriate to trespass somewhat beyond the strict territorial limits of this book, for although Waltham abbey lies just beyond the Greater London boundary it has been closely associated with events in the capital and for centuries exercised considerable influence in the area with which we are concerned. The tradition that I shall briefly relate binds Essex, through Waltham abbey, to the fair western Saxon shire of Somerset. In the attractive village of Montacute there will be found not only the magnificent Elizabethan architecture of Montacute House but one of the legendary shrines of England. Dominating and contrasting with the warm Ham stone of this compact village is the green wooded eminence of St. Michael's Hill, the legendary site of a miraculous event which, it is said, led to the foundation of Waltham abbey. According to the legend a blacksmith of Leodgaresburgh—it was later called Mons Acutus by the Normans—dreamed that Christ appeared to him and bade him dig on top of the hill. Twice he ignored the dream, but on the third occasion he complied and as a result a great crucifix of glistening black flint, together with an ancient bell and an old book, was revealed in the cleft of a rock. When he heard of this, Tovi, who was standard bearer to Canute and lord of Leodgaresburgh and his lands in Essex, hurried to the scene. He had the holy cross placed upon a wagon drawn by twelve red oxen and twelve white cows which, with divine guidance, made their way eastwards across England to Essex, where they halted outside Tovi's house at Waltham. Tovi, thus inspired, erected a church to accommodate the holy cross, to which, according to the tradition, healing powers were attributed.

Earl Harold himself was reputedly cured of paralysis and in gratitude built the great abbey church on the same site. It is said that
prior to the battle of Hastings Harold prayed before the crucifix
of Montacute at Waltham, and some held that it bowed towards
him, thus foretelling the disaster that was imminent.

The Anglo-Saxon era entered its last phase at the accession to
the English throne of the intrepid Harold Godwineson. This was
an event of particular significance to Essex, still fundamentally
Saxon despite its earlier incorporation in the Danelaw. Harold,
who was reputedly buried at the high altar of Waltham abbey,
assumed the monarchy in somewhat controversial circumstances.
Whether or not he reneged on an undertaking given to William of
Normandy will probably never be known for certain. What is clear
is that his increasing influence and power during the last years of
the Confessor's reign had made him the dominant personality in
the kingdom, and at the death in 1057 of Edward the Atheling,
Edmund Ironside's son, the way was clear notwithstanding Harold's
deficiency of royal blood. Edward the Confessor had been closely
connected with Havering, where he frequently enjoyed the peace
and seclusion of this manorial retreat. Harold, who was Earl of
Essex and in possession of several manors in the county, received
the manor of Havering from Edward before the latter's demise and
his name is still preserved in Harold Wood and Harold Hill. The
drama of the critical months of Harold's brief reign overshadowed
the lives of the Saxon communities in south-west Essex, for not only
was he a familiar figure but their future was in his hands. Harold's
position was threatened from the outset by powerful rival claimants,
and the appearance of Halley's comet was taken as a sign of some
portending momentous event. The crisis materialized when he was
confronted by the forces of Harold Hardrada.

The last of the Saxon kings, displaying his characteristic panache,
pursued his seasoned Viking opponents, brought them to bay and
vanquished them in a surprise assault at Stamford Bridge, near
York, on September 25, 1066. Harold Hardrada was killed and the
few survivors of the bloody battle straggled back to Norway in a
handful of the 300 ships in which they had forced their entry into
England via the Humber and the Ouse. But the taste of victory was
short-lived. William of Normandy was poised to make his formidable bid for the English throne and only two days later landed at
Pevensey. By a series of magnificent and resolute forced marches

Harold confronted the Norman chivalry at Battle in Sussex on October 14. His battle-weary and valiant army was defeated in a desperate and heroic day-long battle. Harold and his brothers Gyrth and Leofwine were killed and the Saxon fyrd was finally overcome. The house-carls died at their king's side.

There has been no more decisive event in English history than the Conquest of 1066. London and Essex, as they had in the Roman campaign 1,000 years before, again provided the strategic base on which an invader's authority was founded. Yet again the people of London and south-west Essex felt the iron hand of an alien conqueror. Nowhere else was William's grip so firm. While that impressive symbol of Norman power the Tower of London was being built William established his court at Barking abbey. It was there that he received the homage of the stricken Saxon leaders, among them Edwin and the northern earls Morcar and Thurkil. Edgar the Atheling, who was also present, had already yielded at Berkhamsted. The abbess, Alfgiva, was treated courteously and the abbey confirmed in its rights and properties. It was indeed an essential part of William's political strategy to secure and retain the support of the Church. The circumstances of his birth and of his accession to the English throne demanded that the legitimacy of his claim should be buttressed not only with force but by authority. William's dynamic political activity was motivated by these considerations. Opposition was ruthlessly suppressed by arms. His economic and social dispositions were designed to consolidate his personal position.

The efficiency and extent of the Norman monarchical bureaucracy is impressively revealed in that unique historical document the Domesday survey. These remarkable records were compiled mainly for fiscal purposes, vill by vill, by commissioners of sworn juries comprising the priest, the reeve and six villeins. From them we derive an authentic picture of the status and character of the local communities at the end of the Saxon era as well as at the time of the survey. The concision of its cryptic Latin entries disguises the extraordinary range and wealth of information that the Domesday survey contains and has now yielded to historical research.

It is unfortunate that London was omitted from the survey, but for Essex there is in the so-called Little Domesday a description in considerable detail of the tenurial, economic and demographic circumstances of every manor. In fine we may learn of the fisheries along the Lea at Chingford, Barking, Walthamstow and Leyton; of the eight watermills in the Hams; and of the agrarian economy of the forest communities. On a broader canvas we may discern something of the dramatic impact of the Conquest and the Norman feudal society that flowed from it. The ruthless confiscation of Harold's lands and those of the Saxon thaneage is made abundantly clear. The land grants were probably made soon after the Conquest. At any rate, by 1086, when Domesday was compiled, there were very few English landowners. Most had suffered death, exile or forfeiture. William himself retained about a fifth of the land scheduled in the survey. Of the remainder he left roughly a quarter in the hands of the Church. About half was prudently divided, in widespread estates designed to preclude the consolidation of individual power, among a dozen or so of his principal supporters, such as his half-brother Bishop Odo of Bayeux and Robert of Mortain. This and the rest, which went to the lesser nobility, was held on a tenurial basis that provided the king with a permanent military capacity, for in return for their lands the Norman magnates were required to provide an appropriate number of knights for the king's service. Among the major landowners in Essex were Round's " grasping prelate " Bishop Odo, Eustace of Boulogne, Geoffrey de Mandeville, Peter de Valognes the sheriff of Essex, and Robert Gernon, who held no fewer than forty-four Essex manors, including ones at Chingford, Leyton and the Hams. The king possessed himself of Harold's manor of Havering. The manors at Barking, Woodford, Upminster, Wanstead and Chingford St. Paul's among others in south-west Essex were held by ecclesiastical owners.

Domesday demography is notoriously uncertain, but we may deduce that the total population of Domesday Essex was probably in the range of 70,000 to 80,000. Colchester was the largest town, with 2,000 or so people. The settlements in the forests and marshlands in the angle of the Lea and the Thames were small and probably totalled no more than a few thousand largely engaged in subsistence agriculture. Today the same area supports over 1,000,000 people enjoying the amenities of a highly developed economy. But there is not a parish in metropolitan Essex that does not, in its historical development or topography, bear some mark of the Conquest.

2. Manorial Essex

THE social and economic life of south-west Essex was for centuries based on the manorial institutions—some of which persisted in a modified form into our own times—that grew up in the Anglo-Saxon era and were consolidated and feudalized after the Conquest. It was the Normans who created the administrative apparatus through which William and his successors were able to co-ordinate political and economic policies on a national scale; but at the local level the impact of national events, apart from such as the Conquest and the Reformation, which were profound and traumatic in their effects, was sometimes more apparent than real. Essentially a rural concept, the manorial life of south-west Essex was for the peasant population a seemingly changeless existence. Not until Victoria's time did the span of a common man's lifetime begin to acknowledge that " the old order changeth," for the evolution of modern society was a very gradual process. In its earliest form the feudal system bound all classes together through the interrelationships of personal rights and tenurial and jurisdictional obligations. In brief, in return for certain services, whether owed to the king or to the manorial authorities, a man, be he lord of the manor, freeman or serf, enjoyed defined rights. In modern terms the feudal philosophy is intolerable, but in the less highly organized society of medieval England it placed limits on despotic conduct and provided a basic social stability in what were otherwise turbulent times.

The ruthless decision and political sagacity that characterized William's management of affairs in England enabled him to deal effectively not only with recalcitrant English elements but even with the rebellion of powerful Norman magnates like Bishop Odo and Robert of Mortain. He prudently strove to attract to himself, as king, the sense of loyalty to the Crown of the Church and people which has normally been a feature of the English political scene from Saxon times and without which no sovereign has for long maintained his royal authority.

Throughout the dynastic turbulence and the continental entanglements of Plantagenet, Lancastrian and Yorkist England life in the manorial communities of Essex went relatively undisturbed from generation to generation, with only occasional (though severe) disruptions. Henry II's fatal conflict with Thomas Becket, the crusades and even Magna Charta, which has only assumed its constitutional importance retrospectively, had no conspicuous effect on the slowly evolving life of the area. Perhaps the most noticeable reflection of the fluctuating fortunes of the Crown and the nobility was experienced by the forest communities, whose daily lives were coloured by forest law and custom. John's death at Newark in 1216, only a year after Magna Charta, was followed by the minority of Henry III, war with France and Simon de Montfort's campaign for parliamentary government. Lewes was followed by Evesham and the subsequent baronial struggle with the Crown was thereby prolonged. The people of the Essex marshlands, though not directly involved, were afforded a glimpse of the power struggle that raged above them when Henry III established his headquarters at the abbey of Stratford Langthorne in May 1267 during the last stages of the conflict. Henry's assault on established rights had led to a serious insurrection in London, which was seized by his opponents. Stratford Langthorne was the ideal base from which Henry could lay siege to the capital. The campaign was not prolonged, as the intervention of the papal legate, Cardinal Ottobuono Fieschi, later Pope Adrian VI, resulted in compromise and a reconciliation between the contending parties. As a result Henry entered London on June 18 to resume his kingly authority.

The tempestuous panorama of history unfolded throughout the thirteenth and fourteenth centuries. Edward II's disaster at Bannockburn was later redeemed in English minds by Edward III at Crecy and Poitiers during the Hundred Years War with France. Closely associated with Edward III's policy was a man whose name is prominent in Havering's story, William of Wykeham. Queen Philippa's Hainaulter secretary Froissart, the famous chronicler, wrote of Wykeham's major role in the consolidation of the national fortunes and the rise in the prestige of England during Edward's reign of over half a century. But unpopular taxation, the Achilles heel of political ambition, brought him disfavour and dismissal though not dishonour. The era was marked by two of the most dramatic events of medieval England, plague and the Peasants' Revolt. Contemporary accounts afford grim evidence of the serious mortality which resulted from the Black Death of 1348-9 and subsequent plagues of 1361-2 and 1369. The dire consequences of these visitations which affected the Essex villages did not directly cause, although they accelerated, the erosion of the economic basis of the feudal manorial system and ultimately the decay of villeinage. There was serious discontent in Essex, which with Kent was the scene of the outbreak of the Peasants' Revolt in the midsummer of 1381. The spark that ignited the rebellion was struck at Brentwood by the Thames-side villagers of Fobbing, Stanford-le-Hope and Corringham, who had gone there in force to protest about their taxes. Simultaneously the insurrection flared in Kent. Rochester castle was taken and John Ball released from prison. Manor houses were sacked and manorial records burned. The Essex bands advanced through the Thames-side parishes, crossed the Lea and camped at Mile End and Aldgate. Their demand for the abolition of serfdom, free service, low rents and free markets struck at the roots of the established order of life in the countryside. Led by John Ball, of Colchester, whom Froissart described as " a crazy priest," the Essex rebels, with their Kentish allies under Wat Tyler, threatened the very citadel of feudal England. The rising spread, though less seriously, to East Anglia, the fenlands and even Northumberland. At first the ineptitude of the government allowed the initiative to rest with the angry mobs, who in London liberated the prisoners in the Marshalsea and fired John of Gaunt's palace of the Savoy. The young king Richard II, then only thirteen years of age, confronted the rebellious gathering at Mile End and subsequently at Smithfield. Fired by the canting of John Ball—" When Adam delved and Eve span, who then was gentleman? "—and Wat Tyler, the seething multitude was in an explosive mood. The moment of crisis arrived when, in an unexplained fracas in the presence of the king, Wat Tyler was struck down by the mayor of London, set upon and killed. Richard only retrieved the situation by his cool-headed leadership and by making false promises of concessions and pardons. London and south-west Essex were soon to witness the retribution which, when the impetus of the revolt had subsided, Richard exacted from the peasant population and their leaders in the area. John Ball was executed at St. Albans, and in a speech at Waltham the king vowed " Villeins ye are and villeins ye shall remain." The rebellion in Essex virtually petered out at Billericay soon afterwards, though its embers lingered in the far corners of the county for a while. Whatever the reality of the immediate political situation, the underlying economic factors, strengthened by the effects of the recurring plagues and the revolt, ensured the ultimate collapse of the feudal structure of the manorial system.

By the end of the fourteenth century the economic influence exerted by the capital already foreshadowed the future development of the eventual metropolitan area of Essex. The demand of the capital for foodstuffs, and the growing wool trade, in which the area had a modest stake, led to a move away from the traditional craft industries of rural Essex. By the fifteenth century complementary economic activity in London and south-west Essex had forged indissoluble links between them. Serfdom had almost disappeared, though some dwindling elements of the feudal system survived in the manorial courts and in tenurial practice until the early years of the present century.

On the national plane the futile drain of the French wars continued, punctuated only by the inspiring and prestigeous, but ultimately fruitless, victories of Henry V at Agincourt and Harfleur. The waste of war was pursued at home in the Wars of the Roses, which, high above the heads of a largely apathetic peasantry (and even London was neutral), ended in the triumph of the White Rose over the house of Lancaster in 1461, when Edward IV secured the crown. The Yorkist tenure of the throne was short-lived, for on Bosworth Field in 1485 Henry Tudor wrested the crown from the enigmatic and ill-starred Richard III to found the dynasty which more than any other since Alfred's day epitomized English political genius and martial prowess. The forest parishes of south-west Essex shared to the full the national pride and gusto engendered by Henry Tudor, bluff King Hal and good Queen Bess, with whom they felt more closely identified than with any monarch since Harold.

Through their interest in the chase many of the English kings and queens were familiar figures to the people of the forest area. Barking too, through the abbey, had close associations with the Crown. But it was Havering, where there were two royal residences from the time of Edward the Confessor, that was most closely acquainted with the court. The advent of the purposeful house of Tudor led to strong government, a basic stability and economic growth. The age of the Tudor monarchy saw the continued decline of manorial institutions, the consolidation of royal supremacy, the breach with

Rome and the final abandonment of continental claims. All these were factors in changing and strengthening national life. In the English countryside the era was marked by the development of large estates, the spread of enclosures and the final breakdown of feudal bondage. Henry VII's legacy in 1509 to his only surviving son, Henry VIII, who reigned for the next thirty-eight years, was an established royal authority and national stability. These were the twin foundations on which the Tudor achievement was based. But the affairs of state rarely run smoothly for long, and the age of the Tudors was no exception. The upheaval of the Henrician Reformation, the tribulations of Mary's reign and the Spanish challenge all had to be endured and surmounted. The clash with papal authority was a factor in the growth of English nationalism, and its results were immediately apparent in south-west Essex. In 1538 the abbey of Stratford Langthorne was surrendered to the king by the abbot, William Huddlestone. The dissolution of the abbey at Barking was effected in the following year and of that at Waltham, the last abbey in England to be suppressed, in 1540.

After Henry's death in 1547 the young Edward VI and Lady Jane Grey flitted briefly and tragically across the remorseless stage of history. Essex had good reason to remember their successor, Mary, the old king's daughter by his first wife, Catherine of Aragon, for in the Marian persecutions that strongly radical and protestant county suffered severely. In the churchyard of St. John at Stratford in West Ham there is a memorial inscribed with the names of the martyrs who died defiantly at the stake for their beliefs. The immolation of these men took place at Stratford green before a vast crowd of many thousands, who were inspired by the rare courage and steadfast faith of the victims as they faced the flames. Other burnings took place at Brentwood and Colchester, where one to suffer this ghastly death was a Dagenham man called Christopher Lyster.

But the bleak interlude of Mary Tudor's unhappy reign was as the darkest hour before the dawn. Alfred only excepted, Elizabeth was the most adored and illustrious of England's monarchs. Alfred's unblemished achievements were emulated by the exuberance and brilliance of the Elizabethan spirit which triumphed over adversity and peril. Her charismatic name comes immediately to mind whenever the products of English genius are contemplated. Whether it be in the arts of peace or war, it is to her exultant age that our minds are inevitably drawn. Hers is the name to which the glamour of Shakespeare's, Drake's, Raleigh's and Burghley's is attached. In the annals of south-west Essex the scholarship of Ascham, who was the queen's tutor, and Francis Bacon shed lustre on the Elizabethan achievement. The magnificent Tudor hunting lodge on Dannett's Hill at Chingford bears testimony to the enduring magic of Elizabeth's name in local tradition. She was at Wanstead too, at the home of her favourite, Leicester. From Havering she set out on her great progresses through the eastern counties. From there she went to Tilbury in August 1588 to review and inspire the resolute men of the Essex train-bands who had converged on the port from Colchester and the transit camps at Stratford, East Ham and Romford for the defence of her realm. The warning beacons on Windmill Hill at Woodford had already signalled the appearance of the long-awaited armada off the Lizard. It was not until August 17 that she learned of the calamity that had befallen the enemy's fleet.

London, Essex and all England shared with their great and beloved queen the transcendent joy and thanksgiving for the decisive naval victory over the minatory power of Spain. Only rarely were the queen and the nation, for such the English were by then, divided in spirit. The rejoicing and festivities in the capital on the occasion of the execution in February of the previous year of the scheming Queen of Scots, which brought to an end the prolonged and dangerous issue of Mary's claim to the succession, contrasted with the queen's personal anguish at the act she had for so long sought to avoid. But together they scaled the heights in that glorious hour of England's history when the fleet and its invincible ally, the northern seas, vanquished the formidable armada of Spain.

Despite the crisis over Spanish ambitions, the Stuart succession and the ominous stirrings of the Irish problem, England, guided by the politically sagacious Elizabeth, advanced in wealth and spirit. The exploits of the intrepid English sea-dogs and the flowering of the arts were mirrored by economic enterprise at home and overseas. The Elizabethan age witnessed the steady growth of London as a cultural and commercial centre. The breakdown of feudalism had led to a concentration of government at Westminster. The nation's trade was increasingly centred on London. The capital spread eastwards too from the old city walls along the north bank of the Thames to Stepney. Three centuries later, in another great queen's reign, it was to reach out across the Lea and the Roding into rural Essex.

Essex was in the forefront of the major constitutional and doctrinal issues of the seventeenth century. Endowed with many natural talents, the Stuart sovereigns lacked the basic ingredients of successful kingship, fidelity and political flair. It was thus ironic, and a severe commentary on the house of Stuart, that the British people, wedded as they were to monarchical government, should have attained the height of their prestige during that century under the alien republican concepts of the Commonwealth and the Protectorate. Furthermore, the almost universal joy at the Restoration in 1660 heralded a new and sometimes humiliating decline in British fortunes which was arrested only by the political master-stroke of 1688 which brought the Prince of Orange to the British throne. The capacity of the Stuart sovereigns to invite political disaster was remarkable. Charles I, perhaps the most estimable, died with dignity on the block at Whitehall, and his second son, James II, suffered deposition to make way for " Dutch William " and Mary in 1688. The dour and pedantic James I, with his inability to understand English respect for law, could never fill the void left at Elizabeth's death. Charles II flirted recklessly with the security of his realm, although of all the Stuarts he alone enjoyed moments of real political lucidity and consequentially some brief interludes of personal popularity.

Throughout these vicissitudes of state Essex was staunchly parliamentarian and south-west Essex in particular a stronghold of puritanism. In purely parochial terms the Stuarts were unpopular in the forest parishes because of their abuse of forestal privileges, a circumstance which illustrates only too clearly their political ineptitude. In the forest " rex was lex " with a vengeance. Nor did the salacious personal conduct of Charles II commend itself to the puritanical communities of the area. And there were ship money and chimney money and the unpopular hearth tax to provoke an already offended people. But, as elsewhere, there were some upper-class and clerical families who stood by the king and their old faiths. The Fanshawes, who owned extensive manorial estates in Ilford, Goodmayes and Dagenham, were typical of such. Sir Thomas was heavily fined by Parliament and John Fanshawe's estates were sequestered. Many of the Essex clergy, like John Russell, the rector of Chingford, sequestered in 1644, were forced from their livings and, unlike Russell, were never reinstated. But south-west Essex saw little of the military conflict, for, with London, it was firmly within the sphere of effective parliamentary control.

The most celebrated incident of these precarious times in Essex is the oft-described siege of Colchester, which occurred in 1648 during the bitter struggle of the second civil war. The preliminaries to this episode were witnessed in the area. Defeated by the Round-heads at Maidstone in Kent, a Cavalier force, led by Lord Norwich, retreated over the Thames at Blackwall and was engaged in a skirmish at Bow Bridge. Camping at Stratford, it was forced to fall back along the traditional military route to Chelmsford and Colchester, desultory minor brushes with parliamentary elements taking place at Chadwell Heath and Ilford *en route*. The besieged Royalist forces in Colchester were obliged to yield to Fairfax when supplies ran low and their cause was seen to be lost. The siege ended with the execution of the Royalist commanders Sir Charles Lucas and Sir George Lisle, whose gallant bearing has earned them a page in every Essex history. Colchester bears some of the scars of this dramatic event to this day.

War was not the only calamity suffered by London and Essex in Stuart times. Conflagration and pestilence added to the tribulations of post-Restoration London. The Great Fire of 1666 must have been a compelling, if horrifying, spectacle to the Thames-side villagers, who would have seen the rising smoke by day and the glowing sky at night. They must have been aware, too, of the refugees encamped in the fields at Stepney and Hackney. But their experience in 1666 was vicarious, unlike that of the previous year, when the horrors of the Great Plague were shared with the capital and the Home Counties. Though its social and economic consequences were not as profound as those which resulted from the pandemic of the fourteenth century, the bubonic plague of 1665 has made the greater impact on the imagination. This is at least partly due to the graphic account by Daniel Defoe, who, with remarkable verisimilitude, for it is not history, has described this disastrous event in his *Journal of the Plague Year*. Defoe, incidentally, was descended from an old Essex family settled near Tilbury. Of interest to Greater Londoners is his description of the flight of refugees from London across the Lea into the Essex countryside.

He tells of the difficulties encountered by one party at Walthamstow, where, in common with other Essex villagers, the inhabitants tried to keep the stricken Londoners away. But they failed to prevent the spread of the infection; the villages of south-west Essex from Romford to Walthamstow were seriously affected, as the parish registers show.

At West Ham there were over 150 plague deaths recorded, though we also know that in times of epidemics, which were more frequent than is commonly supposed, the London merchants used the Spotted Dog at Upton as a temporary exchange. Samuel Pepys, spending a few days at Dagnams (a mansion near Romford, not in the parish of Dagenham), passed through Romford, where, he noted, ninety people had died from the plague in 1665. Ralph Josselin, the Puritan vicar of Earls Colne, describes in his diary the fear of countryfolk in Essex of trading with the capital. A great deal of social and commercial intercourse was affected, as people were reluctant to travel. It was, indeed, an offence for a person infected with the plague to venture abroad, such being accounted a felon and punishable by the justices as a vagabond. The Great Plague of 1665 was the last of serious proportions in this country, but its effect on the lives of the village populations of Essex has not yet been fully evaluated by local historians. It would make a valuable line of inquiry.

The cumulative effects of the civil wars, the fire and the plague temporarily retarded the expansion of the capital, which nevertheless played a decisive part in the Restoration of 1660, and twenty years later, in June 1684, Evelyn could write of London " I having in my time seen it almost as large again as it was within my memory." It remained unchallenged as the business and intellectual centre of England, and an emergent middle class was establishing itself in gracious country homes in the pleasant rural environment of the parishes to the east of the Lea. In London the level of population was already imposing a strain on the rudimentary public services. As a result over-population produced slum conditions and health and criminal problems. London's traditional water supplies, drawn from wells, the Thames and the Lea, were inadequate. In 1571 an Act of Parliament had contemplated a channel from the Lea to the city, but the project came to naught and the capital's water supplies were subsequently developed in Hertfordshire by the New River Company. Technically and socially their development was a symbol of change, but eighteenth-century life in the villages and on the manors in rural Essex, despite the developing links with the capital, continued along its evolutionary paths and yet another century or more was to elapse before the manorial chapter closed.

Despite the political debilitation of the Stuart century—war, civil strife, plot, rebellion and intolerance—the flower of English intellectual genius blossomed again. The period between the death of the imperious Elizabeth, the last of the Tudors, in 1603 and the death of the matronly Anne in 1714 encompassed the age of such as Milton, Dryden, Newton, Locke, Wren and Purcell. In a final military flourish the England of Anne gloried in the triumphs of Marlborough's brilliantly conceived and executed battles. Blenheim, Ramilles, Oudenarde and Malplaquet were the pinnacles in this invincible general's European campaigns.

Hanoverian England was naturally an anti-climax, but its pedestrian monarchs at least presided over a kingdom enjoying, and determined to maintain, a stability that had eluded its rulers throughout most of the preceding century. The Commonwealth and the bloodless revolution of 1688 were too close and vivid in English memories to court such risks again. The Jacobite risings of 1715 and 1745 were thus doomed to failure. There would be no return to that unhappy line. Essex, in its traditional religious and political posture, was Hanoverian in its sympathies. Once more, as so often in history, it was aligned with the capital. The Georgian era was to see these affinities strengthened and consolidated.

The eighteenth century was the age of the supremacy of the Whig aristocracy. It witnessed a striking expansion in the scale and influence of the capital which was naturally accompanied by the further development of the rural districts on its perimeter. In some cases, such as Chingford, local geography sheltered the scattered farming hamlets from the direct effects of the growth of the metropolis, but generally villages such as Walthamstow, Leyton, Woodford and the Hams were drawn closer into the capital's orbit. They also served as the country seats of families with London-based businesses. Furthermore, as the resumed upward trend of the population in London and its expanding industries made heavier demands on the products of the area so its role as dormitory and market garden for the capital developed. The landscaped gardens and the fine Georgian houses of the Essex boroughs at Highams and Langtons and along the Woodford ridge date from this period of growth, when the foundations were laid for the unprecedented expansion of London in the nineteenth century.

By then a city of more than half a million people, and the largest in the world, London exerted a dominating influence not only in its immediate area but in the national life and economy. Its cultural and economic activity permeated the whole land. Even in Defoe's time it could confidently be declared that every county in the land supplied the capital with something, be it cheese from Cheshire or Somerset, or cider from Devon. There was fuel, too, from the northern coalfields unloaded from the colliers at Barking creek and taken up the Roding to Ilford. This demand generated growth in agriculture, commerce, industry, communications and shipping. The nation's foreign trade was centred on the port of London; the Thames was its artery. The capital's radiating energies stimulated change also in the social structure and attitudes of the nation. Its power and wealth, for long a decisive factor in national affairs, was further consolidated in this ordered age. The great city was poised to engulf large areas of the Home Counties which were responding to its irresistible demands on their human and natural resources. The principal economic role of south-west Essex was the production of food for the London market. From the Hams to Rainham there was extensive cultivation of vegetables. Potatoes were grown at Ilford and Plaistow, apple orchards and soft fruit gardens were developed at Barking, and dairy farming was carried out in the forest parishes. The Barking fleets supplied the capital's fish.

Towards the end of the century the agricultural prosperity of Essex was undermined by the constraints of the Napoleonic wars, but the effects were less marked in the south-west of the county, where the momentum of the local economies was sustained by the capital's demands, and indeed some industrial development, such as the copper mills at Walthamstow, was stimulated by the needs of war.

The Georgian century was the time of the heyday of vestry government. In the vestry, manorial courts and the justices resided the responsibility for the whole range of local affairs. In them is seen the remarkable continuity of English institutions through centuries of political upheaval and social change. The century saw, too, the emergence of the squirearchy, and though its manorial rights were in the penultimate stage of decline this class played a prominent role in rural society. In south-west Essex the shadow of London now crept across the Lea, and in Chapman and André's map of 1777 we may see a tongue of urban development at West Ham and Stratford. The Thames-side villagers would have witnessed also the increasing commercial traffic on London's river. Defoe states that in a single day more than 2,000 ships could be counted along the Thames and in the Pool of London. Towards the close of the century the population of London had risen to 750,000. An illustration of its unrivalled dominance may be seen in the fact that the next largest town in England, another port, was Bristol with but 60,000 people. In London were concentrated not only the economic sinews of the nation but the trend of fashion and the cultural leadership of life in Georgian England.

The rising tempo of economic activity exposed the weakness of the nation's communications. In Essex roads were bad, though they were worse elsewhere. As long before as 1621 James I, in his irritation at the state of the roads in the county, had issued personal orders for the immediate and effective repair of the main roads at Ilford, Wanstead and Woodford. The poor condition of the roads was often complained of (Defoe and Arthur Young both deplored the state in which they found the Essex roads during their travels in the county), but the vestries, through their appointed and much-maligned surveyors of highways, mostly did as much as their limited resources would allow. The increasing demands of commerce could be met only by a more co-ordinated system with adequate financial arrangements, and this was provided by the turnpike trusts. But aside from inadequacy a further hazard on the roads was the activity of highwaymen, such as Turpin and Everett, which was particularly prevalent in the forest area.

At home, and in Essex in particular, the era was notable for improvements in agricultural practice. This coincided with the enclosure movement and the consequent trend towards larger and more efficient farms. Yet along the western borders of the county open-field and strip-cultivation persisted, examples of this lingering in Chingford and Walthamstow until well into the nineteenth century. The comparative tranquillity of the England of Gainsborough, Kent, Chippendale, Adam, Swift and Johnson provided a contrasting background to the nation's colonial and European involvement. Clive presented his reluctant countrymen with an Indian empire and Wolfe wrested Canada from the French. George III and Lord North were, not surprisingly except perhaps to them, unable to stem the tide of history in North America when the thirteen colonies revolted in 1776. And in little more than a decade after that historic event France erupted in a class revolution which led inevitably to the armed struggle in which Pitt, Nelson and Wellington raised British hearts and prestige to new levels of pride and success. But the strategic consequences of that great conflict, as in all wars, were accompanied by profound economic and philosophical forces which for long inhibited the political life of Victorian England.

3. Metropolitan Essex

THE pre-Victorian years of the nineteenth century in Britain were dominated by the Napoleonic wars and the issue of parliamentary reform. When Bonaparte's France succumbed to the allied armies at Waterloo in 1815 the population of Britain was about 12,000,000. A growing proportion of the people was already urbanized and over 1,000,000 lived in London, which had by then overflowed into Essex. Whereas Wanstead, East Ham, Dagenham and Chingford were still relatively isolated rural communities of barely 1,000 people or less, the populations of West Ham, Walthamstow and Leyton already numbered several thousands. The railways were yet to come, but London had already staked its claim on the area. Its industrial and residential character was taking shape and its people were increasingly newly arrived from East Anglia, the Home Counties and London itself. In West Ham particularly its future identity with Essex was by then precarious. Even in Chingford, where the population total was almost static for most of the period between 1800 and 1850, there was a considerable dilution of the locally born element as a result of the migration of working-class families in search of employment. The changes in social conditions which flowed from the aftermath of the wars were influenced by the philosophies of revolutionary France, the utilitarian doctrines of Bentham and the philanthropy of reformers like Wilberforce, Fowell Buxton and Shaftesbury. But although it was almost another 100 years before universal suffrage was achieved the issue that finally diverted Britain on to the paths that led to democratic government was the Reform Bill of 1832. The agitation for this in fact limited, though significant, measure met with considerable resistance. Its final passage, after the royal assent had been accorded by commission, as the king had refused to attend parliament for the purpose, was accompanied by widespread public excitement. A great feast was held at the Bower House in Havering-atte-Bower. Bonfires were lit in London and the surrounding parishes, and church bells pealed in celebration.

The Act was closely followed by factory legislation and the Poor Law Amendment Act of 1834. One of the first effects of that Act was the abandonment of the Speenhamland system of relief, which in Essex was related to food prices and family circumstances. In practice it also foreshadowed the inevitable end of the ancient system by which local communities were governed. From then on the role of the vestries and the justices was steadily diminished as various other organs of administration were created to tackle the problems of public health and of other local affairs which were beyond the capacity of the vestries.

By mid-century an unprecedented upsurge of national life had gathered momentum. The massive railway building programme, a national factor of the highest importance, was well advanced. The whole pattern of economic and community life was changed by this revolutionary form of travel. Nowhere was the impact more marked than in the London area. The Eastern Counties Railway of 1839 was followed by the Northern and Eastern Railway of 1840 and further routes through south-west Essex. The important junction at Stratford served as the hub for the rail transport system which influenced more than any other local factor the pace and pattern of residential and industrial development in the area. The competition of the railways led to the decline of the canals, but with the improvement of the trunk road routes the infrastructure of a modern economy was laid down in this impressive feat of engineering and organization. The nation's social and administrative capacity was unequal to the strain. Pax Britannica abroad in an age unusually free from war and growing prosperity at home dulled the national senses. The emergence of London as the centre of the world's commerce obscured the existence of the major social problem in the expanding urban area which had been created by the rapid and unco-ordinated increase in economic activity. Thus it was that in

1842 Edwin Chadwick's startling report on the sanitary condition of the labouring population of Great Britain shocked a complacent nation. His description of the ghastly squalor to which many of the people were condemned had a dramatic effect on public opinion. The trenchant prose of this frank Benthamite's report inspired a social crusade which in the literary field was waged in the work of Charles Kingsley and Charles Dickens. " Stagg's Gardens " was all too much of a reality for numerous large Victorian working-class families who lived in squalid rooms and penury. The novelist's brother, Alfred Dickens, a senior official of the General Board of Health, conducted a similar inquiry into the conditions of life in the artisan areas of West Ham with equally disturbing results.

The revelations of poverty and human degradation in these inquiries and the findings of the royal commission of 1843-5 on the problems of town and other populous areas brought to public notice, in a way that demanded action on a national scale, the intolerable conditions in areas which as a result of the industrial revolution had outgrown the capacity of weak and divided local authorities to service them. The royal commissions of 1843-5 and 1868 emphasized the serious deficiencies in the water supplies of the rapidly expanding urban concentrations. Before the Municipal Corporations Act of 1835 there had been no competent authorities responsible for water supplies and other public services. London, by no means the worst case, drew most of its domestic water from the Thames, into which its sewage was also discharged. It was in that context that the Lea valley network of aqueducts and reservoirs was developed from the middle of the nineteenth century.

Meanwhile the population of London and the parishes of south-west Essex had markedly increased. By 1850 there were more than 2,250,000 people living in the capital, and West Ham was poised on the brink of a phenomenal period of development. The newspapers of the time record the depopulation of the farmlands of rural Essex as workers drifted to London and Thames-side as a result of the temporary agricultural depression that set in after the repeal of the Corn Laws in 1846. The industrialization of the area again diminished this problem in south-west Essex, and the fishing industry at Barking was also then at the peak of its prosperity; and when in the 1870s depression again settled on the Essex wheatlands and derelict agricultural land and abandoned farms saddened the countryside the metropolitan area was largely unaffected. Except in the outlying areas its problems were by then related to the social and economic environment created by over-expansion and industrialization.

Although the development of the docks at West Ham from about 1850, the improvement of communications and the upswing in the national economy were the principal stimuli to the creation of metropolitan Essex the process was also encouraged by the local authorities. In London, as part of the attack on the slumdom of the urban perimeter, standards of building and public health were raised and increasingly enforced. This induced industry to move across the Lea, where the local authority was then less stringent, even tolerant, in regard to sub-standard premises and practice. From about 1860 the areas along the Lea and the Thames at West Ham were the main growth points. Navigation on the Lea had been improved and it was toll-free up to Old Ford. The Back Rivers, too, were dredged and banked to provide further access to the new factories. Soap, varnish, match, confectionery, paint, rubber and shipbuilding works were established on the marshlands at Stratford and Silvertown, encouraged by the policy of the West Ham local authority which offered low rates, cheap power and, as compared with London, less inhibiting by-laws. As the railways developed the local industries expanded and spread to other parts of the area. Chemicals and sugar refining at Silvertown and heavy industry at Barking were complemented by concentrations of light industry at Romford, Leyton and Walthamstow. Instrument making and the manufacture of footwear, rubber products, electrical components, wire and cables were also established at Barking, Leyton, Walthamstow and Ilford in the second half of the century. The widespread clothing industry of East London was taken to the Hams, Walthamstow, Romford and Barking. The other important East London trade, furniture and cabinet making, spilled over into Walthamstow. At the same time the area was acquiring the character of a London dormitory as housing estates were developed for local workers and, with the advent of the railways, the growing commuter population. The whole area eventually became an integral part of the Greater London industrial region, which is the largest in Britain, accounting for almost a quarter of the working population in the manfacturing trades. Major enterprises such as the docks, Ford's and power generation fostered satellite industries and thus served further to promote the general development of metropolitan Essex. Simultaneously, public utilities were installed to meet the increasing demands of industry and population. The sewerage and drainage system in the area dates from 1829. In the supply of electricity Leyton was first in the field in 1896. West Ham followed in 1898 and the basic electrical supply system in south-west Essex was established before the outbreak of war in 1914.

The development of land and water communications was vital to the whole process of expansion. Without the Thames there would never have been such a concept as Essex in London. Throughout history it has been the most important factor in the growth of the capital. As far as the Lea was concerned the canal and river system that was developed from 1789 when the New Cut was built was utilized mainly for the carriage of timber and agricultural products from wharfage on the Middlesex and Hertfordshire banks, but it also made its contribution to the growth of industry at West Ham and enabled the British Copper Company to establish its rolling mills at Walthamstow. On land the Victorian century saw not only the birth of the crucial railway system but the steady improvement of the roads and the promotion of passenger and goods services. It was not until the twentieth century that the important trunk routes that now serve the area, the Southend arterial road and the north circular road, were constructed to meet the further demands of commercial and private transport.

The inadequacy of the traditional organs of local government was exposed not simply by the problem of industrialization but by its concomitant the over-population of the urban areas. Dramatic increases occurred in West Ham, East Ham, Leyton and Walthamstow in the latter half of the nineteenth century. By 1900 1,000,000 people lived in the whole of Essex; over 250,000 lived in the county borough of West Ham. The first definite move away from the vestries came in 1834 with the appointment of boards of guardians under the Poor Law Amendment Act. Highway boards and education authorities followed, and in 1856 West Ham became the first of the future Greater London boroughs to appoint a local board of health. By 1890 the same stage had been reached in Wanstead, Walthamstow, Leyton, East Ham, Barking, Ilford and Woodford. Chingford still slumbered in its forest environment. West Ham, developing rapidly, had by 1889 become a county borough, a status in south-west Essex that only East Ham of all the other boroughs was to achieve. Efforts to incorporate West Ham and later East Ham and Walthamstow into London foundered on the anvil of local pride. In London the responsibility for local government was transferred under the Local Government Act of 1888 from the Metropolitan Board of Works to the London County Council.

In the ecclesiastical field Essex was governed from London for well over 1,000 years, forming part of the bishopric of London, but the expansion of London into Essex in the nineteenth century posed new and challenging problems for the Church and made diocesan change inescapable. The whole county, apart from the parishes in the metropolitan area, was thus transferred to the see of Rochester in 1845, but because of the continued growth of the London diocese the future metropolitan parishes were also assigned to Rochester in 1863. A further change took place in 1875, when Essex and Hertfordshire were combined in the diocese of St. Albans. Eventually, in 1914, the county, including the parishes now in the Greater London area, was created as the new diocese of Chelmsford. More recent proposals to combine the metropolitan parishes into a see of Barking would sever a further link with the county, but there are strong historical grounds for re-establishing the spiritual leadership of Barking in the area, as will be seen from what I have written elsewhere in this volume.

During the later stages of the century the domestic scene in Victorian England appears, in retrospect, to have been dominated by the titanic political struggle between William Gladstone and Benjamin Disraeli. Constitutional reform and the liberalization of education and conditions of employment excited the fervent interest of the gradually expanding electorates. The gulf between rich and poor was one of the distinguishing features of Victorian society, as was the emergence of a solid and enfranchised middle class. Beneath the panoply of imperial splendour and the high achievements of Victorian Britain the human tragedy of penurious families and destitute orphans engaged the energies of the philanthropists. Victoria's reign had many facets, and in criticizing the asperities of the social attitudes of her day the work of men like Dr. Thomas Barnardo, whose village homes at Barkingside still care for needy and orphaned children, must be weighed in the balance. The worst aspects of Victorian London were illuminated by his book *Out of the Gutter*, which he published in 1871. In it he described his work in the East End of London searching for " waifs and strays," to whom the traditional benevolence of his now famous homes was extended. Such a problem would seem to defy a permanent solution, but that its existence and the duty of society to deal with it are today recognized owes not a little to Dickens, Barnardo and the other labourers in this field.

Abroad the problems of India, the growing colonial empire and Ireland were the major preoccupation of British politics and consciences. In the arts the highest Victorian achievements were in the literary field, particularly in the comparatively new techniques of the novelist. Dickens, Trollope, Galsworthy and Hardy are familiar names. Tennyson, Macaulay, Ruskin and Carlyle rank among the eminent names of English literature. Kipling, one of the greatest story-tellers of all time, struck an authentic Victorian note. In science the names of Darwin and Faraday were pre-eminent. From metropolitan Essex the work of Lord Lister of West Ham, the famous surgeon, merits the gratitude of humanity for his surgical techniques and the introduction of antiseptics. But amid all this impressive accomplishment the Victorian age was marked by a general decline, though not as disastrous as has been asserted, in æsthetic standards and taste. One who revolted against this was William Morris, of Walthamstow, who championed the cause of craftsmanship and design and whose superb work has survived even the rapidly changing fashions of the twentieth century. He was in the forefront, too, of those who rejoiced in the Epping Forest Act of 1878, by which the lovely forest was saved for posterity. When, in 1882, the queen came to Chingford to declare the forest open and dedicated it for all time to the enjoyment of the public the occasion epitomized much that was inherent in Victorian attitudes and achievement. The denigration of Victorian England is all too prevalent in the condescending attitudes of today. Alongside the urban squalor, the social inequalities and the debasement of public taste are ranged the Victorian virtues of industry, fidelity and humanity. When the Princess Victoria came to the throne in 1837 the monarchy was dangerously low in public esteem. The later Hanoverians had earned the contempt of their people. George IV's ill-usage of Caroline, his queen, was deeply resented in Essex. Victoria's refeshing youth and the rising prestige of her latter years restored the nation to its former allegiance to the Crown. It is still too soon finally to evaluate the Victorian Britain of which metropolitan Essex was a product.

Let us now return briefly to the development of local government in London, for the stage was being set for the Greater London of today. By mid-century local administration had become chaotic in the London area. An administrative jungle of over 300 local authorities grappled vainly with the situation resulting from the rapid and profound changes that were taking place. Some consolidation had been achieved by the Act of 1855 which had set up the Metropolitan Board of Works. Public dissatisfaction with this body led to a royal commission of inquiry and the formation of the London County Council in 1889 under the Act of 1888 by which the county councils, including that of Essex, had been established. London had officially reached the Lea, but it had, as we have seen, in fact already erupted into the green fields of Essex.

At the turn of the century came the consolidation of Essex in London. Although in Chingford and the smaller communities of Havering the major expansion was delayed the future of these areas was settled by the 1930s. The whole area was finally drawn into the ambit of the capital. At Becontree London developed one of the major housing projects in the world and Ford's came to Dagenham. In 1957 a royal commission was appointed to examine the administrative problems arising from the continuing expansion of the capital. This resulted in the London Government Act of 1963 and the formation of the Greater London Council on April 1, 1965. In retrospect, the birth of the five Greater London boroughs in Essex with which this book is concerned seems no more than the inevitable consummation of the process initiated by the Romans 2,000 years ago.

Chapter 3

THE TOPOGRAPHICAL SCENE

THE FOREST

" A certain Territory of woody Grounds "

ARECURRING theme of this book is that of the social and economic identity of south-west Essex and London. Epping Forest, more than any other single topographical feature of the area, symbolizes the affinities between the county and the capital. It straddles what is now the Greater London boundary at Chingford and Woodford, south of which the forest comprises a series of wooded areas and open spaces of varying character and origin. Curving in a gentle verdant arc, it extends some fourteen miles or so from its southern boundary along the foreshore of Victorian London at Newham to the farmlands of rural Essex, into which its topmost tip intrudes just north of Epping. Some have called it London's forest, for it has become the Londoner's country playground and continues, as it has for generations past, to provide an invaluable recreational environment for countless thousands whose homes are immersed in the endless urban acres of the metropolis. But this relatively small though lovely forest is merely a remnant of the great Forest of Essex which once encompassed the whole area and for centuries excited the pecuniary and sporting instincts of the Crown and the nobility. The high royal favour which the forest lands of this part of Essex enjoyed in the past is evidenced by this quotation from Sir Robert Heath which appeared in the Exchequer Bills and Answers of Charles I in 1628:

" A very fertile and fruitfull soyle . . . most useful and com-modious for hunting and chasing of the game of redd and falowe deare . . . alwaies especiallie and above all theire other fforests, prized and esteemed by the King's Maiestie and his said noble progenitors the Kings and Queenes of this Realme of England, as well for his and theire own pleasure and disport and recreation from those pressing cares for the publique weale and safetie which are inseparablie incident to theire kinglie office, as for the interteynment of forreyne Princes and Embassadors, thereby to show unto them the honor and magnificence of the Kings and Queenes of this Realme."

Its attractions as a hunting ground for the English monarchs and their royal guests ensured that the sovereign's rights were jealously guarded, but apart from this the value of the forest as a source of revenue was a principal motive behind the attempts by the Crown to maintain and extend the afforested areas in which it enjoyed rights of " vert and venison." Not only did fines for forest offences make a useful contribution to the royal purse, but there were additionally the rents from assarts and pasturage, the proceeds from the sale of forest produce and a ready supply of venison for the royal table. The forest's history of royal pageantry and splendour is thus overlaid by recurring disputes about jurisdiction, privilege and enclosure.

From at least the seventh century the royal interest in and the control exercised over the afforested areas were never significantly relaxed until the enclosures of the eighteenth century undermined forest authority. Throughout these centuries the story of the forest is that of a perpetual struggle over rights and privileges between the contending interests, the Crown, the forest authorities, the lords of the manors and the commoners of the forest villages. These issues were not finally resolved, as we shall see, until the Epping Forest Act of 1878.

In order to appreciate the nature and purpose of these disputes it is necessary to be clear about the character and status of the forest itself. It is erroneous to think of it as an area of thickly wooded countryside or even the natural landscape as it is today in Epping Forest. Apart from woodland and waste the afforested areas included considerable stretches of cultivated land, villages and even invested small country towns. The concept of the term " forest " was legal and technical, and the areas to which it was applied were subject to the forest laws. This was the crux of the matter and the issue on which so much controversy centred. Sir John Manwood, barrister of Lincoln's Inn and game keeper of Waltham Forest, in his *Treatise of the Forest Laws* originally published in 1592, defined the afforested areas as

" a certain Territory of woody Grounds and fruitful Pastures, privileged for wild Beasts and Fowls of Forest, Chase and Warren to rest and abide there in the safe Protection of the King, for his Delight and Pleasure; which Territory of Ground so privileged is meered and bounded with unremovable Marks, Meeres and Boundaries, either known by Matter of Record or by Prescription; and also replenished with wild Beasts of Venery or Chase, and with great Coverts of Vert, for the Succour of the said Beasts there to abide."

As such the forests were an essential element in the social organization of the kingdom. Within the afforested areas the forest code ensured for the benefit of the Crown the conservation of game, the maintenance of royal prerogatives and the generation of revenue. In Manwood's words again, the forest represented " in its Nature the highest Franchise of princely Pleasure." Pannage and other privileges of the forest population were regulated in the interests of the preservation of the deer. No one was permitted to erect a fence around his property of such a height as to impede the entry of these beasts or to drive them out of the crops, which they were allowed to devour with impunity. The protective measures even went so far as to demand the expedition of dogs, which involved the amputation of three claws from the fore paws, to prevent them from molesting game. The control and management of the forest was thus directed to these ends and rested on the authority of the forest courts and ultimately of the Crown. These courts were the court of attachments (woodmote), which dealt with trivial offences and continued to function until the nineteenth century; the court of swainmote, which heard cases of a more serious nature; and the court of justice seat (or of the chief justice in eyre), which was the superior forest court and operated until 1817. The formal perambulations which were from time to time occasioned by dispute, royal avarice or necessity established the boundaries of the afforested areas and hence the jurisdiction of the courts. The constant struggle over the extent of these areas was at times a political issue of national significance.

The position before the Norman Conquest is to some extent obscure, and there is no documentary proof that the forest lands of Essex were then subject to forest law. However, since the Anglo-Saxon kings enjoyed wide powers over land, afforestation in the later sense as a formal process would not generally have been necessary for the assertion of royal prerogatives. But it is now accepted that the so-called forest code of Canute was a later forgery designed to support the spurious claims of Henry II, and the extent to which the pre-Norman monarchs exercised forest authority is therefore unknown. Despite the dramatic impact of Norman feudalism much of the governmental structure of Anglo-Saxon England survived the Conquest, but in the sphere of forest law there was a considerable extension of regulations and penalties of French origin to which the inhabitants of the forest villages were arbitrarily subjected. Moreover, William and his Norman and Angevin successors brought virtually all the remaining areas of Essex under forest law and the system which they established may be said to have provided the general basis of forest government until the middle of the nineteenth century.

After the death of William resistance to the harsh forest laws arose and fluctuated, with resultant confusion, according to the fortunes of the sovereign and the baronage. The first major forest concession wrung from the Crown was expressed in Magna Charta, three clauses of which (44, 47 and 48) afforded some mitigation of the onerous burden of forest authority. In 1217 Henry III, then in his minority, was obliged to confirm the great charter, the forest clauses being regarded as of such importance as to merit reissue in separate and strengthened form as a charter of the forest. This charter, granted in the wake of the political upheaval which had resulted in Magna Charta and the subsequent civil war, provided for substantial disafforestation and broadly reinstated the forest boundaries as they had been at the accession of Henry II in 1154. Rights of tillage and pannage, very important to the forest villagers, were also restored. Equally significant was the relaxation of the penalties prescribed by forest law. No longer could the killing of the royal deer be punished by death or mutilation, although the non-payment of fines could still result in imprisonment and banishment for defaulters. Another direct consequence of the charter was a formal perambulation of Essex, Surrey and Sussex in 1225. As far as Essex was concerned the boundaries, having been " viewed by good and lawful men," were considerably revised. The area prescribed as royal forest was confined to parts of the south-west of the county. What is now Epping Forest was found to be " within Forest." Havering was Crown demesne; the southern reaches of the present metropolitan area at the Hams, Ilford and Barking and beyond the Ingrebourne was adjudged to be " beyond Forest." But Henry, at the instigation of the chief justiciar, Hubert de Burgh, revoked the forest charter in 1227 on the spurious grounds that it had been sealed by the regent, William Marshall, while he was under ward and not competent to grant it. Henry III thus reversed the disafforestations of Magna Charta and the forest charter. The venison inquisitions made in Essex in 1238-40 confirm that forest jurisdiction extended as far as Colchester and the northern border of the county. By 1250 Henry had recovered much, though not all, of the areas which had been " within Forest " during the reign of Henry II, when afforestation had reached its maximum extent, covering almost a third of the land area of England; but under Henry's eldest son, Edward I, a perambulation of 1301 reversed the trend and the afforested areas were restored broadly to the position at the time of the perambulations of 1225.

The pattern of dispute, perambulation, accession, concession and compromise continued throughout the succeeding centuries, formal confirmations of the forest charter being exacted from Edward I in 1301, Edward III in 1327, Henry IV in 1405 and Henry V in 1416. With the advent of the Tudors, who no less than their Plantagenet predecessors loved the chase, the forest entered a period of royal brilliance, though there is sufficient evidence that its administration was neglected. Henry VII and his grandson, the boy king Edward VI, were frequent visitors to the forest; Mary Tudor and her husband, Philip of Spain, hunted in its ancient glades; but it was Henry VIII and his illustrious daughter by Anne Boleyn who, in history and legend, marked the apogee of royal splendour and pageantry in the forest. They, and indeed all the Tudors, were especially attracted to the Forest of Waltham as it had become to be termed by the early fourteenth century. Henry, who took an intense personal interest in forest affairs, usurped the office of lord warden and made intermittent efforts to enlarge the boundaries of his forests, but the balance of political power in England was changing in Tudor times and he was only marginally successful. Even these acquisitions were surrendered by the Crown shortly after his death. It was one thing to despoil the monastic foundations, but quite another seriously to trespass on the rights of the population at large, noblemen and peasants, in a sphere that affected their lives so closely. Elizabeth, whose name is borne by the splendid old hunting lodge at Chingford, was a passionate and expert huntswoman. One of her chroniclers has averred " Every second day she is on horseback and continues the sport long." Many a splendid scene must have been enacted in the forest during her remarkable reign. Yet towards its end inroads were being made into the established order of the forest; forest law was weakening, and encroachment and poaching posed delicate problems for the forest officials, whose duties had to be performed against a background of public antipathy.

During much of the Stuart era the life of Britain was dominated by dynastic and doctrinal issues of national significance, and forest problems, acute as they were, must be seen in this perspective. The centuries-old struggle about the forestal rights of the Crown nevertheless formed part of the pattern of the political controversies of the age. James I, who was an ardent huntsman, and his successor, Charles I, beset with financial problems, were both active in the rigorous assertion of their rights over the forests. Efforts were made by the latter to extend the forest boundaries for revenue purposes following the refusal of supply by Parliament. Another problem was enclosure of forest wastes, which had never been wholly prevented.

James I made a shrewd move in establishing a commission in 1620 to survey and sell enclosed land, and thus turned to pecuniary advantage a situation which the forest authorities could not wholly control. By the same process landowners were able to obtain a secure title to disputed land.

Along with ship money and general taxation the extension of the forests was a cause of popular grievance. It was said in James's reign that it was safer to kill a man than a deer! Their scant respect for private rights and ownership earned the early Stuarts a deserved unpopularity in the forest areas. Juries were coerced into imposing unjustified fines for offences which it was alleged were revived under obsolete forest laws in areas which had been disafforested throughout living memory. Opposition was particularly strong in Essex, and this led to the perambulation of 1641, which more or less stabilized the legal position until the nineteenth century. In south-west Essex the forest boundaries were redrawn broadly along the limits established in 1301 apart from the exclusion of the liberty of Havering. The lands of the present Greater London boroughs were, as a result, within either the forest or the purlieus, which were marginal areas in which, although not forming part of the forest, certain forest laws applied.

Administration during the Commonwealth and the Protectorate was lax, and the condition of the forests deteriorated to such an extent that after the Restoration Charles II had to take remedial measures for the rehabilitation of the herds of deer. But an even more serious danger than neglect threatened the forest in 1653 when the Long Parliament legislated for its disafforestation and sale. This process had already begun when Oliver Cromwell took the matter out of the hands of Parliament and referred the problem to an inquiry by special commissioners, but their activity too was terminated by the Restoration in 1660. Charles regularly visited the forest on hunting expeditions and for more nefarious pursuits, but after his reign royal interest in the sporting attractions of the forest waned. Under pressure from public opinion Crown rights were slowly eroded and in some instances abandoned altogether. The forest also gained a bad reputation for lawlessness when gangs of outlaws, many of whom were discharged soldiers, roamed the wastes attacking and robbing unwary travellers. Matters were so serious that it even became necessary to pass an Act of Parliament to deal with the forest gangs, of which the Waltham Blacks were the most notorious. John Byrom, writing in 1728, described the forest, by then referred to as Epping Forest, disparagingly thus:

> " *Thro' the wild brakes of Epping Forest lay . . .*
> *. . . a dreary landscape, bushy and forlorn,*
> *Where rogues start up like mushrooms in a morn.*"

The Waltham Blacks, incidentally, adopted their name not from the Essex town but from Bishop's Waltham in Hampshire. The deer stealers in Waltham Chase, Hampshire, reputedly blackened their faces when operating at night and thus arose the term applied to lawless gangs in other forest areas of England.

It is interesting to note that in 1793 the land revenue commissioners, in reporting on the unsatisfactory state of the forest, emphasized the environmental importance to the metropolis of these undeveloped tracts of country and advised against enclosure, which had, for all practical purposes, virtually acquired the mantle of policy. But the pressures were increasing, and abuses in the early nineteenth century were rife. Not only enclosure but the removal of gravel, sand, turf and timber, as well as deer stealing, was common practice. In 1805 the Crown, setting the tone, enclosed and sold the forestal rights of the manor of West Ham. By 1850 the 9,000 acres recorded by the land revenue commissioners in their report of 1793 had been reduced to about 6,000. The forest courts, although they had maintained their authority far later than elsewhere, had by then ceased to function and forest officials had largely lost control of the situation. Even the lord warden of the Forest, the Hon. W. Pole-Wellesley, enclosed forest lands and sold the rights he had been appointed to uphold. All this was done in the name of progress and the utilitarian philosophy of the day. Arthur Young, in his study of agriculture in Essex, had viewed the forest as an unproductive and intolerable nuisance. The attitude of the Crown lent respectability to the actions of the local landowners. The selfish and dismal process was described by Sir Walter Besant with devastating irony:

" They converted miles of wild forest, with rough uplands and green dales covered with grand old trees, into a treeless tract, staked out in square fields and rectangular roads. Then they wagged their stupid heads, and rubbed together their ridiculous hands, and said it was a great improvement."

Hainault Forest, part of the remainder of which lies within the area and responsibility of the Greater London Council, also fell victim to the assault on the surviving areas of the forest. In 1851 an Act was passed effecting the disafforestation and enclosure of this beautiful enclave of the ancient forest. In a swift operation much of the forest land was cleared before public indignation could be brought to bear. Farther afield the New Forest and the Forest of Dean were similarly threatened. Public opinion was now thoroughly aroused, parliamentary interest was mounting and the tide had begun to turn. In 1865 the Commons Preservation Society was founded and played a major role in co-ordinating the campaign, which then acquired the strength and direction that were eventually decisive in stemming and finally reversing the process of enclosure.

Public support for the struggle, in which powerful forces were then engaged, was further intensified when, like so many other popular movements, it was presented with its martyrs. In March 1866 the Willingale brothers, together with William Higgins, were brought before the police court at Waltham Abbey and charged with and convicted of malicious trespass on property as a result of their exercise of the right of lopping. Refusing to pay the fines imposed, they were committed to jail at Ilford. The Willingales' father, Thomas, had previously been arraigned before the court for the same reason, and the family was again involved in similar proceedings in 1872. The plight of these robust Loughton villagers focused public attention on the issue, and although the cases were never finally decided time and purpose were gained and the stage was set for what was to prove the most important and far-reaching case in the field of litigation over commons in the legal annals of England.

That London and Essex can still share and relish what remains of Epping Forest is due not only to the spirited tenacity of the Essex villagers in asserting their ancient forestal privileges but to the decisive and public-spirited action of the Corporation of the City of London in intervening in the legal battle. Its competence to do so derived from the commoners' rights which it enjoyed on account of the ownership of some 200 acres of land in the forest parish of Little Ilford at Wanstead. The great case against illegal enclosure opened in July 1871, and as a result of this costly litigation the corporation secured the verdict which saved the forest and led to the Epping Forest Act of 1878. In a brilliant exposition of the case and his judgment the Master of the Rolls, Sir George Jessel, pronounced in favour of the corporation on all the main issues, granted an injunction against future enclosures and ordered the return to the forest of many earlier enclosures.

Under the Act of 1878 the corporation was appointed as conservator for the surviving 2,000 acres or so of the forest and a considerable amount of formerly enclosed land which was restored to it. Altogether some 5,500 acres were secured, to which have been added important acquisitions in the Greater London area such as Highams Park in 1891 and Yardley Hill in 1899. The present chapter of the story of the forest was formally opened by Queen Victoria on the occasion of her visit to Chingford and High Beech in 1882, when she dedicated Epping Forest to the use and enjoyment of the public for all time.

In this brief survey of the history of Epping Forest we can see that it is shared not only by all the Greater London boroughs of Essex but by the capital and the county as a whole. The Greater London areas of the forest now lie within the boroughs of Waltham Forest, Redbridge and Newham. Within these boroughs are the forest parishes of Chingford, Walthamstow, Leyton, Woodford, Wanstead, Little Ilford and West Ham. The other five forest parishes still lie over the Essex border. Each of these parishes retains the traditional mark by which the commoners' cattle are identified. Fair numbers of cattle are still to be seen in the Greater London parishes, mainly at Chingford Plain, Yardley Hill and Woodford Green, although they also find their way down to the flats at Leyton and Wanstead, where there are other good grazing grounds. The right of commoners to graze their cattle in the forest was confirmed by the Act of 1878, and although there are complaints from time to time and agitation for the withdrawal of this privilege, on account of the damage caused to private property by straying animals, their departure from the local scene would be generally regretted. The existence of these free-ranging herds enhances the rural aspect of the residential areas that border the forest. There can be few London suburbs to day where cattle still make their ponderous way through forest-side roads in the early morning, with little disturbance of the slumbering populace, as they regularly do at North Chingford and elsewhere in the area. The presence of these animals is consistent, too, with the conservators' objective of maintaining the natural aspect of the forest, which apart from the former grounds of the great house at Wanstead is in no sense parkland and is entirely unfenced.

So successful have the conservators been in preserving the natural appearance of the forest that the casual visitor is not conscious of the scientific and management problems that arise from its proximity to the vast urbanized area of Greater London. Those problems have been contained if not solved, and, as recent field studies have shown, it is remarkable how the wild life of such areas as Epping Forest has not only survived but has even learned to exploit the conditions created by an urban environment. The expansion of London and local communications has destroyed many of the natural habitats and disturbed the ecological conditions in the area, but although there has consequentially been a reduction in the range of birds and animals now resident in the forest districts there seems

to have been little impoverishment of wild life in general. Many of
the birds of the forest and smaller animals such as squirrels, rabbits
and hedgehogs have thrived in a situation that might have been
expected to threaten their survival. Grey squirrels may be seen in
almost every part of the forest and, as is common experience elsewhere, have driven out the more attractive red squirrels, although
a few of these may still remain. The forest still provides a natural
habitat for badgers, foxes, hares and stoats, though not in sufficiently
large numbers to invite comparison with earlier times when wild
boars, wild cats and wolves ranged the heaths and woodlands of
the royal forest. But the pride of the forest has always been the wild
deer that once thrived in abundance in the aura of royal favour. At
one time red and roe deer were plentiful as well as fallow, but the
enclosures of the seventeenth and eighteenth centuries led to a
serious diminution in their number and when the City corporation
assumed its duties in 1878 there were no more than about twenty
or so of the unique herd of black fallow deer still in the forest. One
of the tasks of the conservators is to preserve the purity of this herd,
strictly speaking dark brown rather than black, which means that
strays from outside have to be closely controlled. In 1883 E. N.
Buxton introduced some roe deer into the forest from Dorset, but
the experiment failed and they gradually died out. By 1917 none
remained. Meanwhile the conservators, through careful management, largely re-established the black fallow and by 1900 several
hundred head were recorded, but modern conditions have resulted
in a further depletion. There are now no more than about seventy,
if that, and they are becoming more and more confined to selected
areas.

Each spring on the forest ponds the broods of cygnets add a
delightful touch to these popular beauty spots. The mute swan is
said to be indigenous in the London area, but whether this is true
of the feral swans in the forest it is impossible to say. Many have
been introduced from elsewhere and domesticated from time to
time. On rare occasions hooper swans have been noted at Connaught Water, Chingford, but the last occasion was some years
back. In England swans have a niche of their own in our social
history, for, like the forest deer, they were once jealously guarded
for the sovereign, to whom they were deemed to belong unless

maintained under manorial privilege. Lovely as they are, the protection afforded to them was, alas, for no higher purpose than the royal table, for which they provided a delicacy and a welcome source of fresh meat. Specially appointed officials regulated and protected the royal swan population, aided by a code of law and practice. The ceremony of " swan-upping," at which the young birds were counted and marked, still survives on the upper reaches of the Thames, which once teemed with these elegant creatures. Royal rights lapsed generally about 200 years ago, although they are still enjoyed by the Crown and certain of the City livery companies on the Thames. Unhappily, the malicious molestation the forest broods have suffered in recent years has resulted in the loss of nests and eggs, but swans are game and pertinacious birds and still stick to their haunts on the local ponds at Wanstead, Leyton, Theydon Bois and Chingford.

That the forest has been sadly denuded of wild flowers must, as with the deer, be laid largely at the door of progress. The depredations caused by the ever-increasing number of visitors and changes in natural conditions in the area have meant the loss of many species that once graced the forest. Whereas there used to be seen bluebells, primroses, wood anemones and other exquisite wayside flowers in some profusion there are now few places in the forest where they can be found in any quantity. Even the ubiquitous bluebell, which once flourished at Chingford and in the Walthamstow Forest, is now mainly confined, except for Wanstead Park, to a few areas beyond the Greater London boundary. The trees of the forest, however, are in better condition now than in 1878 because lopping came to an end with the Epping Forest Act and the pollards have grown on to a spectacular maturity. The skilled management and control of the forest has also encouraged regeneration. There are, nevertheless, no stands of great antiquity, for forest timber was taken in the past not only for domestic purposes but for naval construction. Large quantities were cut in Pepys's day, when the logs were rafted down the Thames from Barking creek to the royal dockyards. It was not until well on into the eighteenth century that the forest ceased to be a source of timber for the fleet.

The finest woodlands in the forest are on the Essex side of the border on the undulating terrain of the Monk Woods and in the Epping Thicks, but some attractive wooded areas and fine open countryside are to be found in the forest boroughs, particularly at

Chingford. In the Greater London areas the forest comprises mainly oak and hornbeam, although the other principal trees of the forest are also present. Hornbeam is one of the trees with which Essex is particularly well endowed. Epping Forest is in fact one of the most important hornbeam areas in Europe, and there are other sizeable woods in Essex in which this tree is dominant, notably in Hatfield Forest and at Blake's Wood just east of Chelmsford. Hornbeam is a splendid timber, as hard and durable as oak. Though fairly tolerant, it flourishes on the heavier soils in the lower parts of the forest and can be seen to good advantage in Hawk Wood and Bury Wood at Chingford. It is interesting to note that in the past hornbeam was invariably used for the cogs in the gearing mechanism of windmills as well as for pulleys and tools and other industrial purposes where very hard wood was necessary. Oak, of course, is pre-eminent as a tree and as timber and is present in most parts of the forest. The special uses to which the woods of other trees in the forest were put in the past is also of interest. I can mention but a few. The blackthorn, which blooms so excitingly in the early spring and is plentiful in the area, was in great demand for hedging and for walking sticks. The holly provided an excellent wood for inlay work and for the handles of riding whips. In the southern areas of the forest it may be noted that holly thickets are more in evidence than elsewhere, not only because the trees thrive on the drier soils but because they are not there subject to the browsing of the deer, which are rarely seen south of Chingford. There is a splendid avenue of limes leading up Dannett's Hill from the station at Chingford to the hunting lodge. This was planted when Ranger's Road was cut in 1880 to link Chingford with the main London to Epping road. The Saxons used lime wood for their shields because of its lightness and durability. One of Woodford's most conspicuous features is the long roadside border of horse-chestnuts, which are at their best in the spring when the cream blossom illumines the main road through the old village. Because of its resistance to insects chestnut was greatly favoured as a building timber, particularly in churches, for which it was much used in Essex, where there is a lack of suitable stone.

It is only to be expected that an area so rich in historical associations should also enjoy an abundance of legend. Thus to the natural delights of London's forest may be added charming if unverified tales of the English kings and queens whose personal lives were so closely linked with it. The earliest of these legends credits Edward the Confessor with a charitable act that was said to have given rise to the name of Havering, where the king maintained his favourite country seat. According to this tradition a beggar to whom Edward had given his ring proved to be none other than St. John the evangelist, who eventually returned the ring to the king by the hand of an English pilgrim whom he encountered in the Holy Land, with the message " Have ring." This pleasant fiction was represented in medieval religious art and may be seen depicted in a window in Romford parish church.

Anne Boleyn is the best remembered of Henry VIII's queens, and during her brief, ill-fated courtship and marriage with the Tudor monarch was a frequent visitor to the Forest of Waltham. Anne was not to be rushed into the royal nuptials after the death of her young fiancé and prevailed upon the king to permit the customary period of mourning to elapse. High in royal favour, she was regaled with gifts, including, if legend is to be believed, a brick-built tower at East Ham, later called Anne Boleyn's castle, from which the queen-to-be could scan the green vistas of the Essex meadows, the forest and the river panorama of the Thames. The forest legends do not neglect the tragic finale of the young queen's dalliance with the Crown. They tell of Henry waiting in the Forest of Waltham for the sounds of gunfire from the Tower of London that would announce the execution of his second consort and thus make way for the third, Jane Seymour, who in turn was to die prematurely at the birth of Edward VI. Henry is reputed to have ordered the day's hunting to begin as soon as the fateful signal was heard. He was not the man to allow remorse to inhibit his enjoyment of the forest; and was not the delectable Jane already in contemplation? This poignant scene is placed at High Beech and at Pimp Hall, Chingford, which was once in the possession of Henry VIII, though not at the time of Anne Boleyn's death.

It was perhaps fitting that the only child of this ill-omened union was to raise the prestige of the house of Tudor to its highest levels and that the most famous legend of Elizabeth in the forest should tell of triumph and not disaster. Who but pedants and professional " debunkers " would not wish to accept the authenticity of the stirring occasion on which, so tradition asserts, Gloriana mounted the fine oak staircase of the hunting lodge at Chingford on her white palfrey in her elation on receiving the news of the famous sea victory over the Armada of Spain in 1588? Although built before her time the lodge rightly bears her name, for it symbolizes the Tudors' love affair with the royal Forest of Waltham, which they drenched with history and legend. The Stuarts too have left their mark on forest tradition, for, as we shall see in the annals of the modern borough of Waltham Forest, the knighting of the sirloin of beef by Charles II—or was it James I or Henry VIII?—holds pride of place among local legends.

There are legends also of highwaymen which embellish the sordid activities of these ruffianly characters with an aura of romance. Dick Turpin, who relied for much of his success on the collusion of certain forest innkeepers, was born in 1705 at the Bell inn at Hempstead in north Essex and became the scourge of the forest area. He came to London at an early age and was apprenticed to a butcher in Whitechapel. Later he lived at Plaistow and East Ham for a time and married a local girl called Hester Palmer. Turpin embarked on a career of smuggling, highway robbery and murder, and his infamous reputation dies hard in the forest area, where he had hideouts at Sewardstone, High Beech and Hackney marshes. This evil man is also known to have frequented the Spotted Dog at Upton and the Green Man at Leytonstone. He was eventually caught and hanged at York. According to contemporary accounts he faced his end with courage, and this no doubt explains the unmerited favour with which his legendary exploits have been recounted. Two other notorious " gentlemen of the road " were John Everett and his accomplice Dicky Bird. The forest roads were never safe in their day, but they both came to the same squalid end as Turpin—on the scaffold. Bird was executed at Chelmsford and Everett, in 1730, at Tyburn, on which occasion the latter appeared dressed in the finery, with gold watch and chain, silver snuff-box and bejewelled signet ring, which were presumably trophies of his more successful period. It is an extraordinary and unexplained fact how he managed to retain the spoils of his trade, but it might, I suppose, be attributable to the spurious prestige that has always attached to these infamous villains.

★   ★   ★   ★

Let us now turn to the more agreeable associations of the forest area. The connections between Essex and the thirteen colonies which were eventually to form the United States of America are many and well known. Essex has contributed its full share to the human and architectural heritage of that great nation. We are all familiar with the tragic epic of the Billericay villagers and the settlement of the *Mayflower* community in Maryland. The links between the Penn family and Wanstead and Walthamstow and between General Oglethorpe and Cranham will be mentioned elsewhere in this book. Lawrence Washington, the great-great-grandfather of George Washington, was rector at Purleigh's delightful hilltop church and is buried in St. Peter's at Maldon, where incidentally Christopher Jones, the captain of the *Mayflower*, was christened. But an interesting and not so well known fact, which has always intrigued me, is that the first American president's mother was known as the "rose of Epping Forest." George Washington was born in 1732, the eldest son of Augustine Washington and his second wife, Mary Ball, of Epping Forest, Virginia. The Ball homestead, where Mary was born in 1706, had been so called by her ancestors, the only logical explanation being that they had themselves originated from that part of Essex or at least known and loved it sufficiently to wish to perpetuate its name in the new world in which they made their home. The house stood near the mouth of the Rappahannock River where it broadens into the beautiful Chesapeake Bay. Unfortunately only a few of the original outbuildings of the farm remain, but they deserve to be a place of pilgrimage for any visitors from the forest boroughs who chance to be in Virginia. Mary was evidently one of the belles of colonial Virginia if her picturesque sobriquet is a true reflection of her youthful charms. Orphaned at fifteen, she married Augustine Washington at twenty-two and there is some possibility that their courtship had blossomed in England, but this cannot be verified. I wish I had had sufficient leisure and opportunity to delve further into this fascinating topic of forest lore. It remains an unclaimed minor prize for some local researcher with the time, inclination and luck to ferret out the answer.

It is almost impossible to contemplate the forest in its lighter moods without recalling the delightful poetry of the puckish Tom Hood, who lived at Lake House in Wanstead during the early 1830s. A contemporary of John Clare, who was also closely associated with the forest, Hood was among the best-known poets of his age. Like the unfortunate Clare, Hood's sojourn in the area was not in the happiest circumstances. Dogged with ill health and financial difficulty, he was compelled to withdraw from the local scene but he left us some effervescent verse. His special " gimmick "—as we would say nowadays—was his outrageous use of the pun: " I need to be a lively Hood to make my livelihood! " and " The Easter Chase will soon be numbered with the pastimes of past times: its dogs will have had their day and its deer will be fallow. A few more seasons and this City Common Hunt will become uncommon."

It is Hood's narrative poem about the Easter chase for which we should be most grateful. The rollicking stanzas of *The Epping Hunt* should be read by all who enjoy the forest. Published in 1829, with illustrations by George Cruickshank, it is laced with humour and garnished here and there with delicate touches wherever the author's lyrical instincts surface, as in the verse

> " *And lo! the dim and distant hunt*
> *Diminished in a trice:*
> *The steeds, like Cinderella's team,*
> *Seemed dwindling into mice.*"

More of this anon.

Hood's verse is as good an introduction to forest literature as we shall find, for he invariably strikes the right note. Beautiful and historic as it is, the mood of the forest is frequently tempered by informal gaiety and spontaneity, and Hood's poetry is never lacking in either of these qualities. He was not alone in finding inspiration in the forest. It is not surprising therefore that a number of notable poets were born or bred or made their homes in the forest villages from which the populous Greater London boroughs have developed. They have endowed us with a wealth of pastoral literature which one day an enterprising author and a benevolent publisher will present to a fortunate public as a forest anthology of a rare variety and richness that have never yet been fully appreciated. In this parnassian galaxy the forest area is represented in the age of Elizabeth by the self-styled " Green Knight," George Gascoigne of Walthamstow, his stepson Nicholas Breton, whose delicate verse can charm even in this meretricious age, and Thomas Lodge of Leyton, who was born at West Ham in the year of the great queen's accession. They were followed in the seventeenth century by the philosophical and sombre George Herbert of Woodford and the prolific Francis and his son John Quarles of Romford, whose talents earned them a popularity of surprisingly long duration. Coventry Patmore, something of a moralist and a minor Victorian poet, was born at Woodford. But a high-water mark of Victorian culture was reached in the fields of art and literature by the versatile genius of William Morris. He and his followers imposed new standards of refinement on much of the everyday life of an age not generally notable for its taste and sensitivity.

William Morris, who was born at Walthamstow in 1834, was inspired throughout his life by youthful memories of the forest he loved and knew " yard by yard from Wanstead to the Theydons and from Hale End to the Fairlop Oak." No more sensitive eye ever scanned the forest scene, which to him had a " peculiar charm of its own not to be found in any other forest." Long before he died Morris deplored the inroads made into Epping Forest and despaired for its future. He would, I suspect, be agreeably surprised if he could see the forest today and how successfully, despite the pressures of the twentieth century, the tidal waves of modern urban development have been resisted. He would be on familiar ground in the small but genuine area of forest at Walthamstow and Gilbert's Slade, and would delight in the thrilling avenue of horse-chestnuts at Woodford Green, where cricket is still played by the local club as it has been on this part of Epping Forest for over two centuries. The fine panoramas at Chingford Plain, rescued from the plough but still bearing the furrowed evidence of enclosure, would provide worthy material for even William Morris's demanding pen.

The broad flats and the ponds at Leyton and Wanstead lend distance and character to a local scene which might otherwise have receded into suburban oblivion. The views across the Lea valley from Yardley Hill and Pole Hill have a quality and range uncommon in Essex, where scenery generally relies on high skies and broad horizons rather than on altitude and escarpment. Below Chingford's green hillsides lies the Ching rivulet, which, rising from Connaught Water, empties into the Lea just south of Cook's ferry. One of the most delightful walks in Greater London is along the track of this forest stream, which for part of its course forms the boundary with the county as it crosses Chingford Plain. After this it meanders through woody groves to Whitehall Plain, an old drift-way through which the commoners' cattle used to be driven to their grazing grounds when this part of the forest was enclosed. Beyond Chingford Hatch, below Friday Hill, the Ching drops away through Hatch Forest and The Lops, passing Highams Park and on to the Lea. As I have already mentioned, the only part of the forest that may be described as parkland is at Wanstead. Here the ordered green pleasance of the former grounds of the great mansion affords an attractive enclave at the southern end of the forest crescent. The ornamental lakes, the grotto and the bluebells in spring give Wanstead Park an individual character that distinguishes it from the grassy plains and the woodland areas of the forest that stretch intermittently northwards and the broad acres of Wanstead Flats that lie immediately to the south.

At the Hollow Pond on Leyton Flats or the pretty little Bullrush Pond by the Rising Sun and at the traditional forest fairs we can still recapture some of the atmosphere of gaiety of the forest festivities and the Epping hunt of bygone days. The Epping hunt was a popular and democratic event in which all classes joined annually, on every conceivable conveyance and on foot, in the hilarious pursuit of a beribboned stag through the forest. There was seldom any serious intention of harming the wretched animal, which was stabled at Woodford by a certain Mr. Rounding—Tom Hood's " jovial elf "—and released specially for the event. The hunt originally enjoyed royal patronage, but had degenerated into a farce and a public annoyance by the time the last attempted revival at High Beech was frustrated by the police in 1882. I have already alluded to Hood's highly amusing poem about the Epping hunt, in which the antics of the hapless John Huggins and the uninhibited attitudes of the participants are described in such captivating verse. These examples should be more than enough to tempt the reader who has not so far enjoyed his first reading of this local ode.

> " *Now Huggins, standing far aloof,*
> *Had never seen the deer,*
> *Till all at once he saw the beast*
> *Come charging in his rear. . . .*

Trees raced along, all Essex fled
Beneath him as he sate,
He never saw a county go
At such a county rate! "

The forest fairs are sophisticated occasions nowadays compared with those of the past, but the essential attributes of communal zest and informality are still present. The continuity of these fairs justifies a slight digression at this point, for they occupy a minor niche in our social history. Nowadays fairs are organized for fun and profit, but they used to serve more serious purposes as well. Nearly always associated with church festivals, they were of considerable economic utility, attracting traders from home and abroad. Alongside the festivities the transaction of business at fairs was an important element in the trading relationships between town and country. Fairs were also a source of revenue, for from the twelfth century they were regulated by the grant of special—and lucrative—jurisdictions conferred by the king, the sponsors levying tolls and dues under licence. The forest holiday fairs are thus the inheritors of an institution of great antiquity. A local example was the fair that was established by charter in 1465 and held annually up to the late eighteenth century on Ascension Day at Havering Green. But the best remembered fair of the forest area is that which used to be held at Fairlop.

The Fairlop fair was founded by Daniel Day, who was born in Southwark in 1683 and was the owner of a small estate at Hainault. An eccentric extrovert, Day used to visit his estate on the first Friday in July for the purpose of collecting the rents from his tenants. He invariably took the opportunity provided by this occasion to entertain his friends, whom he regaled with beans and bacon under the spreading canopy of the Fairlop oak in Hainault Forest. This annual function developed into the Fairlop fair, and long before Day's death had ceased to be a private affair. The oak itself had a girth of thirty-six feet and was virtually destroyed by fire in June 1805, the gutted trunk finally yielding to the elements when it was blown down by a gale in February 1820. A new oak tree was planted by the Prince of Wales on May 22, 1909, on the reputed site of the famous tree at the London playing fields ground in Hainault Forest. The timber from the old tree still survives, for from it was fashioned the pulpit of St. Pancras church. As for Day himself, he died in 1767 and was buried in a coffin also made from a bough of the celebrated oak. Memories of the Fairlop fair and of the Epping hunt conjure the authentic flavour of the forest in its traditional role as the Londoner's playground, and these events are the genuine social antecedents of their modern counterparts.

On any sunny weekend the forest roads are still thronged with pleasure-seeking Londoners making for their time-honoured haunts at the various forest centres. Although they pursue their pleasures in a modern idiom they are animated by the same instincts as their forebears. The forest is there to be enjoyed; it is part of the life of London and its roads still offer the most beautiful of all the numerous approaches to the capital. In the mind's eye the swift, noisome flow of traffic today gives way to a rural past, when the forest roads were cluttered with droves of Essex cattle which, with flocks of geese from Norfolk and the trundling haywains, were driven through the forest villages to London before the railways created a new age. No longer does London welcome the wagoners rolling into town from East Anglia and the north, their horses gaily bedecked with mayblossom gathered in the forest from the long-lived hawthorn. They have given way to brightly coloured, glistening cars and coaches whose occupants scarcely notice the blossom as they speed through the last few miles of London's countryside before plunging into the drab urban morass of East London which has almost, but not quite, engulfed the lovely forest with which the capital has shared so much of its history. But if London has imposed itself upon Epping Forest the forest has impressed its own character upon the Greater London boroughs that gratefully embrace the southern reaches of this sylvan landscape. It would be hard to imagine and impossible to contemplate Essex in London bereft of " a certain Territory of woody Grounds."

Chapter 4

THE ARCHITECTURAL HERITAGE

THE presentation of any topographical theme imposes a duty on the author to convey at least a broad general impression of his chosen territory. The difficulty of so generalizing about such a varied area as Essex in London is, however, particularly apparent in attempting a survey of its architectural character. It has for centuries been subjected to the pressures of competing influences: the continuing expansion of London, industrialization, the break-up of the manorial estates, the forest and the receding agricultural periphery. Broadly speaking, it is to these influences that the general appearance of the modern boroughs can be attributed. Despite the impact of the industrial and technological revolutions during the last 200 years there remains in the boroughs an impressive array of buildings of genuine antiquity. These should not be preserved merely for their antiquarian virtues, for that is at best a limited concept of their value. Their real merit resides in the cultural and æsthetic contribution which they make to contemporary standards so frequently debased by dreary box-like megastructures that pose as modern architecture.

Much of the Thames-side and Leaside boroughs now bears the decisive imprint that industry has imposed. Adjacent to the older industrial areas are residential districts characterized by the monotonous terraced streets of a decaying Victorian townscape. Row upon serried row of tiled and slated roofs spread outwards and around the railways and industrial installations. Here is the visual evidence of what results when standards are subordinated to "progress." Towards the forest and the rural boundaries of Redbridge, Havering and Waltham Forest we find areas of typical twentieth-century suburban development. In all the boroughs the urban scene is relieved here and there by picturesque fragments of their village nuclei and isolated buildings representative of the Tudor and Georgian periods in the life of the Essex countryside before it was overrun. These buildings—the churches, manor houses, farmsteads and country seats—help us to visualize the character of the area in former days. Some of the most impressive of the buildings of Essex in London have long since disappeared. Nothing but the foundation plan of the great cruciform abbey church remains at Barking, the famous abbey of Stratford Langthorne has vanished almost without trace, and so too has the splendour and opulence of the vast Palladian mansion at Wanstead. But the architectural capital of Essex in London, if sadly depleted, is by no means exhausted, as we shall see.

Anyone at all interested in local history or our architectural heritage when visiting a town or village goes first to see its church. No other building is so eloquent of the life and history of a local community, and there is no church in the land in which there will not be found something that is either beautiful or interesting. In Essex the parochial organization of the Christian Church was well established before the Conquest and many of our parish churches had Saxon predecessors. Here and there in rural Essex are traces of work from this period, and there are also two outstandingly interesting and evocative Saxon churches at Greensted and Bradwell. In metropolitan Essex there is nothing remaining from Saxon times apart from a fragment of sculpture located in St. Margaret's at Barking. This small section of the shaft of a Saxon cross, a rarity in Essex, was discovered in 1911 built into the churchyard wall. It is carved on all sides with elaborate interlaced circular patterns typical of late-tenth-century ornamentation. It was almost certainly associated with Barking abbey, and it has been suggested that it dates from the tenth century, when the abbey was refounded by Archbishop Duncan after the defeat of the Danish invaders.

If this ancient carving is all that survives from Saxon Essex in the buildings in this part of the county, Essex in London is otherwise surprisingly rich in the quality and diversity of its ecclesiastical architecture. Where else can be found in such proximity two superb examples of Norman church buildings like those at East Ham and Rainham? The hilltop churches at Upminster and Chingford and the elegant St. Andrew's at Hornchurch occupy commanding sites and are representative of the various phases of the Gothic period, of which all the London boroughs can provide examples comparable with the county as a whole. And if there is little in the parish churches in Essex to match the Norman edifices of the Thames-side boroughs there is certainly nothing to rival the Georgian architecture of St. Mary's at Wanstead now that Mistley is despoiled. Even the Victorian revivalists, for all their deficiencies, managed to reserve some of their better work for metropolitan Essex.

The main distinguishing features of the Norman period are the semi-circular arch, the massive column and the various chevron, lozenge and zigzag designs which embellish Norman stonework. In Essex there is a good deal of fine Norman work, especially in the military architecture at Colchester and Castle Hedingham and the superb nave of Waltham abbey. Probably half of the medieval churches in the county contain some feature of the period. Among the best are Rainham and East Ham, the latter being similar in plan to Copford and Hadleigh, which are among the outstanding Norman churches of Essex.

Visitors to St. Mary Magdalene at East Ham will observe that the church is constructed on the plan of the Roman basilica, and although the tower dates from the sixteenth century the remainder of the building exhibits the authentic characteristics of the Norman period. The charming twelfth-century apsidal chancel, framed as it is in a simple semi-circular arch of lovely line and proportions, should be specially noted. St. Helen and St. Giles at Rainham is a rare example of an almost complete late-Norman church. Its dedication too is rare, there being no other church in Essex dedicated to St. Helen. This is a surprising fact in view of the legendary, though unfounded, association of the mother of Constantine the Great with Roman Colchester. The robust shafted square piers and narrow deep splayed windows at Rainham pronounce inescapably the Norman origin of the building. The scalloped capitals of the arcade and the typical zigzag decoration of the chancel arch are emphatic. Here is an architectural jewel clothed in the mellow patina of time. Indeed, there is so much of interest to engage one's attention in this church that it must be quite difficult to concentrate on any but the most stimulating sermons. But this hardly explains the self-denigration of the somewhat eccentric curate there in 1756, Charles Churchill, who in writing of his own preaching confessed " sleep at my bidding crept from pew to pew." Only the diagonal buttresses of the tower and the south aisle betray subsequent gestures to the Gothic enthusiasm of later centuries in this unambiguous Norman fane.

Most of our English churches are built in one or more of three main classifications of the Gothic style which epitomizes the popular view of ecclesiastical architecture. In metropolitan Essex there is a full range of examples from the Early English onwards. The immediate impact of the Gothic style on the emotions contrasts strongly with the effort required to appreciate the classical, to which we shall come shortly. The intimate appeal of a beautiful Gothic church like St. Andrew's at Hornchurch makes no demands on the intellect; it is lovable at first sight. This light and spacious parish church is one of elegant proportions. It dates from the thirteenth century, though tradition places the origin of the church at Hornchurch in Saxon times. The present structure is mainly of the fifteenth century, but, as in so many of our medieval churches, there was much restoration carried out in the last century. Apart from the general architectural merits of the church there are some interesting details which should not be overlooked. These include a memorial high up on the north wall of the chancel carved by John Flaxman, a precocious and talented artist of East Anglian descent, much of whose work graces Westminster Abbey and St. Paul's, quite apart from his numerous private commissions in the churches of the Home Counties. The Hornchurch memorial, to one Richard Spencer, was carved in 1784 and comprises two angels on either side of a central medallion and portrait. Other and later examples of Flaxman's work in Essex in London may be seen at St. Mary's, Leyton, in the Hillersdon and Bosanquet memorials. Another interesting object at Hornchurch is the restored figure at the top of the stairs of the fifteenth-century tower which is said to represent William of Wykeham. The most intriguing figure of the church, however, is the rebus on the gable at the east end of the chancel in the form of a bull's head with prominent horns. There have been various explanations offered about this and the name of Hornchurch itself, none of which is entirely satisfactory.

Among the best viewpoints in south-west Essex are the hilltops of Chingford. From the lovely medieval church of All Saints on Chingford Mount there is a panoramic vista across Waltham Forest and the Lea valley to the City of London. On a clear night the great dome of Wren's glorious cathedral dominates the horizon beyond a galactic sea of twinkling lights. The modest village church is perhaps the most charming and assimilable in the Essex boroughs. It is a very good example of a small country church with architectural features of the thirteenth to sixteenth centuries. In its fabric it is in the tradition of the Thames-side parishes, where the churches are often built of Kentish ragstone, which could be transported on the rivers. Conversely, the parish church of St. Laurence at Upminster belongs generically to that range of buildings in the "timber" areas of the county. Half hidden in the conifers of its tree-clad churchyard, this secluded church, though much altered in the last two centuries, is enhanced by a fine timber-framed tower the lower stages of which date from the early thirteenth century. The nave arcade is contemporary with the tower, or possibly a little later, exhibiting features of the transitional period.

Let us turn now from the exciting architectural vocabulary of the generally anonymous masons who fashioned our medieval churches to the classical excellence and disciplined restraint of the Georgian builders, among whom Wren, Gibbs and Inigo Jones are familiar names. Although there is very little to note in Essex by these illustrious practitioners they imposed standards of a high order on their age. The church at Wanstead was built in 1789 by Thomas Hardwick in the classical style of the period and consecrated in the following year by the Bishop of London. It is the epitome of good taste and the white Portland stone of the building is most becoming set amid the greenery of its immediate environment. The church is dedicated to St. Mary the Virgin, a distinction it shares with more than a quarter of the 400 or so medieval churches of Essex. The exterior is graced by the Doric porch, which is supported by columns of the Tuscan order. Capping the roof-line is a neat classical turret and cupola constructed with pairs of Ionic columns at each corner. The interior is enriched by tall Corinthian columns which carry the graceful arches of the nave. The galleries, box pews and Jacobean pulpit are noteworthy. The restrained hand of its Georgian designer is in evidence in all aspects of the building. Nothing is overdone except perhaps the monument to Sir Josiah Child and his three wives, which, dating from 1699, is not of the same period, although it is generally regarded as a fine example of baroque sculpture. Sir Josiah was a director of the East India Company and a merchant banker. The monument, which was transferred from the earlier Gothic church, is in black and white marble and was executed by John van Nost. I personally prefer the tasteful proportions and gentle classical inflections imparted to the church by Hardwick to the more extravagant creation of van Nost, but the Child family is interesting and if you can stomach baroque here is the best in Essex.

In a rapidly developing area such as south-west Essex in the nine-teenth century there was naturally a demand for more churches of all denominations to meet the pastoral needs of the growing com-munities. We thus find, in all the boroughs, many churches which date from that period. Generally speaking the neo-Gothic churches of that phase of our architectural history were not notable for their artistic merits, since they lacked the spontaneity and inspirational qualities of their medieval prototypes, but occasionally an architect with the courage of his convictions rose above the grey uniformity of his contemporaries. The church of St. Peter and St. Paul at Chingford Green was basically the work of Lewis Vulliamy, but by great good fortune was completed by one such Victorian, Sir Arthur Blomfield, who was responsible for a number of other public buildings in Essex, among them Bancroft's School at Wood-ford Wells and St. John's, Colchester. The result was a most satis-fying piece of architecture because of, rather than despite, the bold and intelligent blending of the revived Early English and Perpen-dicular styles in which the architects worked. Vulliamy built the church in 1844 and Blomfield's competent enlargement was carried out in 1903. It is a fine example of Victorian Gothic, with vigorous flushwork in flint and, since the extension, pleasing proportions. Well sited on the old village green, the church was erected at the expense of the rector, the Rev. Robert Boothby Heathcote, who was also the lord of the manor of Chingford Earls, as a replacement for the lovely old church on the Mount, which then resumed its former dedication of All Saints. I shall mention but one other of the many churches of this vintage in the area, that of St. Edward the Confessor at Romford. John Johnson built it in the market place, an historic corner of old Romford, in 1850. The dedication appropriately acknowledges the local tradition of this enigmatic Anglo-Saxon king, whose connections with Havering are described later in this volume.

Before turning to the secular buildings of the area it is perhaps apposite to dwell for a moment on an aspect of ecclesiology which is of artistic as well as historical relevance. In the churches of Essex in London there is extant an excellent range of sepulchral brasses well up to the standards of the county, which with Kent is pre-eminent in quality and quantity in England. Currently in vogue, representations of these attractive and historically valuable items of antiquity nowadays appear on the market in various artistic media. Brasses originated in Germany and first appeared in England about the middle of the thirteenth century. They are commonly found fixed in matrices on church pavements, though sometimes they may be elevated on altar tombs.

The earliest remaining monumental brass in England is at Stoke D'Abernon in Surrey and dates from 1277, though there are records of a few others of previous dates. Often of high artistic merit, they are of value to historians for the detailed information they yield on genealogical problems and the development of armour and costume. Among the brasses to be found in south-west Essex are those in Rainham's Norman church, already described, where there are several late-fifteenth-century examples, including the only one in Essex to portray tilting shields. At Hornchurch there is a rare brass inscription, and in St. Laurence, Upminster, a very interesting palimpsest brass on which effigies of Nicholas Wayte and his wife have been cut over an earlier memorial to an ecclesiastical dignitary, possibly a bishop. There is also a good early example of 1502 at North Ockendon depicting William Poyntz in knight's armour.

Brasses illustrating the development of civilian costume can be seen at Barking (Broke, 1493), Walthamstow (Monoux, 1543), West Ham (Stapels, 1592) and Leyton (Tobias Wood, 1620). Most precious in the rich harvest of Essex brasses is the superb late-fifteenth-century example in St. Peter and St. Paul at Dagenham which commemorates the Urswyck family of the manor of Marks. On a rather small scale for such a large group of figures, it is of outstanding quality and visitors will find the delightful study of Sir Thomas and Lady Urswyck and their nine daughters of absorbing interest and charm. Sir Thomas himself was a lawyer by profession and held the appointments of Chief Baron of the Exchequer and Recorder of London. The commemorative brass of 1479, which will be found on a tomb chest in the chancel, depicts Sir Thomas in legal garb. Dame Ann is adorned with a glorious jewelled necklace and a spectacular " butterfly " head-dress of the period, as befits a lady with such a bevy of charming daughters. Fittingly grouped, with hands clasped in supplication, the Urswyck daughters are headed by one in sombre religious habit. In contrast, the others, with delightful grace, wear remarkable head-dresses of a conical steeple type which I believe are unique on English brasses. If I may tentatively suggest that the hunting lodge at Chingford and the smock mill at Upminster are at one end of the spectrum of the most beautiful and interesting objects in Essex in London, large and small, this little memorial is certainly at the other.

In secular architecture the principal buildings of the boroughs of Essex in London make a worthy contribution to the varied and comprehensive range for which Essex is justly renowned. Unique, for there is nothing quite comparable elsewhere, is the fine forest lodge at Chingford. Because of its associations with the capricious Tudor queen it has long been known as Queen Elizabeth's hunting lodge, though it was built before she came to the throne. This robust timber-framed lodge, which must be acknowledged as one of the showpieces of metropolitan Essex, exudes the appeal and atmosphere of age. It originally served the purpose of a " standing " from which the monarch and her courtiers watched the hunting of deer across Chingford Plain. The documentary evidence is inconclusive, but in all probability it was finished in 1543 as part of the work commissioned by Henry VIII in establishing a royal park at Fairmead. It was expertly restored about seventy years ago and is of very considerable architectural interest. The massive timbers, especially in the generously contrived open roofwork, are of the same structural quality as the work of the Essex carpenters who built the sturdy, rugged frames for the timber towers of churches like those at Blackmore and Navestock. Among its specially interesting minor features are the enclosed staircase well and the slightly cambered flooring on the upper stories, where the joisting was cut and arranged to facilitate the run-off of rainwater when the lodge served its original purpose as an open stand. The legends about Queen Elizabeth I and the lodge are part of the romance of Epping Forest. Legend, too, about connections with the Gunpowder Plot lingers around another handsome building of the period, Eastbury House, which stands embedded in a modern housing estate just off Ripple Road at Barking, its red brick harmonizing generously with its humbler neighbours. Architectually it is a significant example of its type and there is no mistaking its vintage. The clustered twisted stacks, its balanced H-plan proportions, regular fenestration and red-bricked gabled frontages stamp it as a classic example of a late-

Elizabethan manor house and an important building in Greater London's architectural inventory. An unexpected gem in the suburban stratum, the house does much to relieve the tedium of Barking's featureless acres.

Before we leave the new borough let us pause for a moment to contemplate the spacious Valence House in the park of the same name at Dagenham. The building is basically timber-framed with lath and plaster infillings, though it has been much developed during the last two centuries. The oldest parts of the house are in the centre of the present structure. The west wing was added in the eighteenth century and some further alterations were made when it was taken over as council offices. A few miles to the east of Upminster there are also two attractive houses of the timber-framed type. Great Tomkins and Upminster Hall. The former, by Upminster Common, stands in trim gardens today but was once no doubt the home of a prosperous yeoman farmer. It still retains some of its original fifteenth-century features and its well-preserved exposed timbering is typical of the eastern counties. Upminster Hall, now a golf club, is noteworthy for its conspicuous multi-gabled elevations and, like its neighbour, has an integral hall of Elizabethan type.

The period from 1715 to 1830, which covers roughly the phase which for convenience we may call Georgian, though of course it embraces the Regency, saw an efflorescence of architecture in England comparable with the high noon of the Gothic centuries. Unlike their medieval predecessors, the Georgian designers were bound by canons of taste, symmetry and classical composition. An exposed flying buttress or a pointed arch would have been intolerable; the appeal was æsthetic and intellectual, never emotive; the purpose to charm rather than to inspire. With the expansion of the national economy, by then firmly based on London, the period saw a marked increase in the building of substantial private residences within reach of the capital. The Georgian buildings of Essex in London today are the precious legacy of that spacious age.

The glory of the area, and indeed of Essex, was Wanstead House, designed and begun in 1715 by Colen Campbell, a contemporary of Gibbs and Kent, for Sir Richard Child, later the first Earl of Tylney and son of Sir Josiah, to whom I have already referred. This vast mansion was built in the classical style of the sixteenth-century Italian architect Andrea Palladio at the cost of over £300,000. This no doubt contributed to its sad and untimely end. The vicissitudes of the owners indeed make a depressing chronicle of the fall from opulence to insolvency. Eventually the house was demolished and sold piecemeal by the creditors in 1824 after its owners had been reduced to penury, and so Wanstead lost its magnificence. Nothing now remains *in situ* except the gateposts bearing Sir Richard's cypher which stood at the entrance to the grounds now maintained as Wanstead Park by the conservators of Epping Forest. The pediment is preserved at Hendon, and some of the pillars from this noble building may still be seen in West Ham. They were used to form a portico for a meeting house in North Street where famous Quakers such as the Gurneys and Elizabeth Fry used to worship. The portico now forms part of the drab outbuildings of a college of further education. I wonder whether these once proud columns will yet be rescued from the oblivion of their present poverty.

We must return to the present and the best Georgian house in the area today, Rainham Hall, a relatively modest country mansion of 1729 which stands next to the church of St. Helen and St. Giles. Square and undemanding, this delightful house exhibits the minimum of classical detail on its red-brick and intelligently related frontages. The overall restraint in decoration allows the splendidly carved oak Corinthian porch to be displayed to full advantage. The house is fronted by wrought-iron railings and gateway of obvious vigour and fine craftsmanship. It was built as a private residence for Captain John Harle, who ran a wharfing business at Rainham Creek. It is now maintained by the National Trust and Rainham and Essex can therefore rest assured of the safety of this Georgian gem. This is a house to be enjoyed.

Rainham Hall, for all its cultured charm, is but an isolated survival. If we wish to experience some of the full flavour of the London environs of Georgian Essex we must seek it at the other end of the area. Well within the limits of a not too strenuous afternoon's walk one can savour a whole range of Georgian buildings sited along the forest ridge at Woodford and Walthamstow. This Georgian perambulation starts at Hart's Hospital at Woodford Green. One of the hospital buildings, now used as a nurses' residence, dates from the end of the period and has a typically coherent Georgian façade with an integrated Ionic colonnade. It stands on the site of the house built in 1617 for Sir Humphrey Handforth, master of the wardrobe to James I. There were at least two other distinguished occupants: " silver-tongued " Onslow, a notable Speaker of the House of Commons, and the botanist Richard Warner. Farther south on the opposite side of the green is Highams, standing just over the Waltham Forest border. This prominent Georgian manor house, now a girls' high school, exudes the grace and taste associated with the age. It dates from 1768 and is notable for having been landscaped by Humphry Repton, who lived for many years at Romford. The famous Repton " Red Book " illustrating his proposals is at the Walthamstow museum on loan from the Warner family, who were the last owners of the manor. The manor house was earlier situated at Higham Hill, but this site was abandoned in favour of the commanding position which the present house occupies close by Woodford Row. This elegant house was designed for the lord of the manor, Anthony Bacon, M.P. for Aylesbury, by William Newton and was originally symmetrical. Additions were made in about 1785 for the Hornbys and by Repton in 1790 for John Harman. It is most gratifying that the latest extensions carried out by the Essex education authorities in 1928 and 1938 harmonize so well with the older building, which now forms the central block. The splendid views across the Ching valley which were admired by Repton have changed, but the retention of a large part of the old grounds has ensured that the building remains in a most attractive setting.

A little farther on, at the top of Salway Hill, is Hurst House, which Nikolaus Pevsner dates from 1714 and describes as " the best house of Woodford." It certainly has an excellent front elevation graced by striking Corinthian pilaster columns and orthodox classical motifs. The house was once gutted by fire but was reconstructed in 1937. It is undeniably a fine building, but it is not well sited and does not blend out of context as easily as so much less conscious Georgian building so often does. From here to Gates's corner there are a number of other fine houses of the period, the best being the delightful Old Rectory just south of the parish church. I have always regarded this elegant eighteenth-century house as the most attractive of all the municipal buildings of metropolitan Essex, rivalled only by Langtons, which since 1929 has been used for public purposes by the Hornchurch council and latterly by Havering. The Woodford office, now a court, belonged to the church, having been built as a replacement for an earlier rectory in about 1710. As we see it today the house bears the appearance of a later phase, having been partly reconstructed at a subsequent date.

It nestles in small but charming grounds, at their best in the fall, when the autumn-tinted foliage blends prettily with the house. For a while in private ownership, it was acquired by the Woodford Urban District Council in 1934. The appeal of the house is the refinement and simplicity of its late Georgian façade, which is a model of architectural discipline. Another house of merit in the same group is Elmhurst, which although appearing somewhat austere at first sight has some interesting detail, and closer examination will be found rewarding. What a superb half-mile this must have been before the other Georgian houses, including Grove Hall, Frithmans, Ivy House and The Roses, were demolished.

Our afternoon excursion is by no means ended, for our route takes us on to Snaresbrook and round by the immaculate White Lodge. The quiet charm of this exquisite little Georgian house has won many hearts, and I am grateful to the owners, who a little time ago were kind enough to show my wife and me over it and its pleasant gardens. Just beyond the Eagle Pond we stumble upon a pretty, and unexpected, corner of Walthamstow at the Forest School, where will be found an elegant row of Georgian houses sited advantageously along the edge of Epping Forest. That is perhaps enough for most to manage between lunch and tea, but there is in fact much more of the period to be seen in the borough. Inconveniently dispersed, but worth the effort, are the interesting Water House of 1762 with its symmetrical convex bays, the charming Brookscroft and the Vestry House, now the Walthamstow museum. The latter was built in 1730 as the workhouse and is modestly handsome.

In the new borough of Havering, apart from Rainham Hall, there are Langtons, a mid-Georgian house of distinction, and the excellent Bower House at Havering-atte-Bower. Langtons was bequeathed to the Hornchurch council and is charmingly sited amid lawns and flower beds and an ornamental lake, all of which must be preserved unaltered under the terms of the bequest. The Bower House is earlier, having been built by Henry Flitcroft in 1729.

No résumé of Victorian architecture, however brief, can fail to include a reference to the work of Gilbert Scott or some other member of his prolific family. His major contribution to this area was the orphan asylum, now the Royal Wanstead School, of 1843 at Holly Bush Hill, which provides such a pleasing backdrop to the Eagle Pond. Its cultured features lend style to the symmetrical grey and buff stonework. The Jacobean idiom of this agreeable building is typical of Victorian efforts to revive traditional styles, and it now forms a familiar and admired landmark beyond the lake at Snaresbrook. But of course the whole area has much, ecclesiastical and secular, that dates from the age when the railways and industry were transforming its entire character. Large residential areas, especially in Newham, Barking and Waltham Forest, are virtually undiluted relics of that expanding era. Many of the public buildings are Victorian, and though often dull and unimaginative they display a confident, if slightly fussy, dignity. Essex in London has its fair share of these monuments to past municipal pride, not wholly emulated by their pretentious Scandinavian-style successors of the twentieth century. Good examples of the latter are the civic centres at Dagenham and Walthamstow, which stand white and incongruous in the hearts of these otherwise plebeian localities.

Now a new generation of building is making its impact on the face of metropolitan Essex. Today, from vantage points like the flats at Wanstead and Leyton, there can be seen modern multistoried Manhattan profiles thrusting above the forest skyline to complete the remarkable range of buildings that spans eight centuries in the life of Essex in London. There is indeed much more that could be described, for I have naturally dwelt on the best or most representative buildings. There remains in the area something for all tastes, as I have tried to show: the Norman and Gothic parish churches, the timber-framed survivals of Tudor England, elegant Georgian country houses and architectural Victoriana. Without these priceless survivals the identity of this corner of Essex would have been wholly submerged in London and the twentieth century.

The Royal Wanstead School

Chapter 5

A TOPOGRAPHICAL MISCELLANY

of cotes and mills and stocks and stiles ...

IN the last chapter we surveyed the fine churches and splendid houses that still grace the London boroughs of Essex. Often less conspicuous, but of much interest and charm, are the lesser objects of antiquity. Tucked away in odd corners of Essex in London the percipient traveller will find the surviving emblems of a rural background and other objects deserving of a place in a topographical study of the area. The delightful Tudor dovecote at Chingford is symbolic of the manorial past; the superb smock mill at Upminster epitomizes the agricultural tradition; a fire-mark at Rainham is a minuscule token of a crisis in London's story. This chapter is concerned with such buildings and objects which a casual visitor might so easily overlook.

Standing prettily at the foot of Friday Hill in Chingford, secluded in the lee of a fine row of elms, is the sixteenth-century dovecote which was one of the appurtenances of the ancient manor of Pympes. Together with the timber-framed barn the cote is a picturesque survival. The timber frame of the building is constructed on a red-brick plinth, the infilling comprising lath, plaster and brick nogging. No longer do voracious flights of pigeons flutter from the louvre of the gently pitched pyramidal roof to devour the crops of a resentful local peasantry. The dovecote now serves the mundane purpose of a store for the local authority, which has developed the old farm as a nursery, and presides serenely and usefully over the unmolested crops of the allotment holders and municipal gardeners.

The importance of the dovecote, pigeon house or columbarium—call it what you will—in the manorial economy and the intrinsic interest of these buildings justifies a further digression at this point. The numerous great round and richly decorated columbaria in France will be well known to continental tourists, but it is not always realized that they are not uncommon in England, where there is a variety of styles exhibiting period and regional characteristics. There still remains a fair number in Essex too. The origin of the dovecote takes us back at least as far as the Romans, who domesticated the pigeons that were fattened for the table. Roman historians have described in detail the methods of breeding and rearing these birds, a particular delicacy for the Roman epicure being young birds stuffed with spices and partly masticated bread. Although the Romans in Britain undoubtedly indulged themselves in the luxury of pigeon meat there is no evidence of their use of cotes, which were probably first introduced into this country by the Normans. It is virtually certain, however, that the domesticated pigeon was unknown in Saxon Britain, since there is no mention of pigeons or dovehouses in the Domesday survey, which nevertheless recorded such minor appurtenances as beehives. But the Saxons knew of the merits of pigeon meat, which they obtained from the wild wood-pigeon, believed to have descended from the domestic birds of Roman households. Incidentally, the Old English word for these wood-pigeons was *culfre*, from which is derived the terms culver and culver house which used to be employed instead of pigeon and pigeon house. Nowadays the term is met in minor place and road names, such as Culver Field and Culver Lane, and generally indicates the site of a lost dovecote.

The Normans housed their pigeons in nesting holes in the walls of the castle keep, the earliest extant example of this being Rochester, which dates from 1126. The earliest references to individual dovecotes occur in documents of the early thirteenth century. The first Essex reference is to a dovecote at Feering in 1289. That pigeons provided a regular source of fresh meat in medieval England is well established, but they had other uses too. The Romans used them as message carriers and in later times there was a superstitious belief that the flesh was a protection against the plague and various physical ailments. In his diary entry of October 19, 1663, Pepys tells of Queen Catherine, Charles II's ill-used Portuguese spouse, then dangerously ill, receiving extreme unction and having " pidgeons put to her feet " and precious relics upon her head. To which of these measures may be attributed her recovery on that occasion is a matter for conjecture. The queen herself graciously and properly credited this to the king's prayers.

Pigeons were also a source of social dispute, and the dovecote was the all-too-familiar symbol of the authority of the lords of the manor over the subordinate classes, for only the lords of the manor and other privileged persons were permitted to keep these birds. The law governing this was repealed in 1825, by which time agricultural progress and social changes had so altered the situation that it was no longer needed. Previously the deprived peasantry had additionally to suffer the depredation of their own crops by the vast foraging flocks of domestic pigeons maintained by the favoured few. One observant Elizabethan traveller remarked that " no kingdom in the world hath so many dovecotes " as England, and in John Milton's day there were estimated to be some 26,000 cotes in the country. With each averaging several hundred pairs the scale of the problem that afflicted the peasant farmers can be imagined. The seventeenth-century lawyer John Selden, to whom Thomas Fuller, the estimable cleric of Waltham Abbey, refers as " the learned Mr. Selden," wrote in his *Table Talk*: " Conscience. Some men make it a case of Conscience, whether a man may have a pigeon-house, because his Pigeons eat other Folk's corn. But there is no such thing as Conscience in the Business; the Matter is, whether he be a Man of such Quality, that the State allows him to have a Dove-house; if so, there's an end of the Business." Small wonder that manorial court documents frequently record the presentment of villagers for illegally trapping the lord's pigeons with nets and various other ingenious devices.

The dovecote at Chingford and a number of others remaining in rural Essex are but the last of the numerous cotes that were once scattered throughout the countryside. In the area of Essex in London they were as common as elsewhere. Some, notably at Stubbers, North Ockendon, Corbet's Tey, Goodmayes, Padnall Grove Farm at Ilford and Cranham Hall, survived until comparatively recent times.

Another familiar profile in the English countryside, now, unhappily, rare except in a few areas of eastern England, was that of the windmill. These exciting buildings have a special fascination, and even the most hardened travellers are exhilarated by the spectacle of a full-sailed mill responding bravely to the wind. Conversely, there are few more depressing sights than a forlorn, derelict and sailless mill crumbling under the winds that it once defied and harnessed in the vigour of its youth. At one time there were several thousand windmills in England, mainly in the windswept, low-lying areas of the eastern counties. They were common in Essex and a fair number were to be found in what is now the metropolitan area. The mills in England still working now number no more than a score or so. In Essex in London, representative of the smock mills that we associate with southern Essex and Kent, there remains only the splendid hilltop mill at St. Mary's Lane, Upminster.

Ever since man first cultivated corn there have been mills of a sort. From the simplest roughly fashioned manual grinding stones has evolved the electrically operated milling machinery of the twentieth century. But it was the windmill alone that combined æsthetic with technical satisfaction. Alas, these queens of the countryside have been dethroned. Their place has been usurped by " King Pylon." Our present-day Don Quixotes have tilted in vain at these metallic giants that stride at monotonous intervals across forest, down and pasture. Unlike the windmill, which draws its power from invisible currents in the air, these modern props, for they are no more, drape their clustered cables across an offended skyline.

As far as is known, the earliest windmills were used in Persia in the tenth century, but they were not introduced into Europe until the twelfth. The first Essex reference is of 1202 to one at Henham in the north-west of the county. The first mills in England were post mills, which, as the name implies, rotated on a central post so that the sails were positioned to make the most effective use of the prevailing wind. A mill known to have existed at Barking in 1242 was almost certainly one of this type. Other early references to windmills in south-west Essex are found for Romford and Hornchurch in 1249, Havering-atte-Bower in 1262 and East Ham in 1307. Like the dovecote, a mill of one kind or another was essential to the manorial economy. In feudal England the lord of the manor held monopolistic rights in milling. Many a man kept an illegal hand-mill hidden away in his cottage, but on the whole the unfortunate villagers coerced into using the lord's mill had to pay for the privilege. Here too was an inevitable field for dispute in the manorial courts. It was, it is true, sometimes possible for a tenant to obtain permission to build and operate his own mill, but there were restrictions imposed on this and in certain circumstances rights over the mill and even the ownership would revert to the lord of the manor. Even the most pertinacious litigants rarely prevailed over the established or arrogated rights of the manor. One local example, at Barking, was when the abbess brought a successful action against the Dun brothers, William and Geoffrey, who had erected a windmill on lands over which she enjoyed privilege from the Crown.

Along Thames-side on the low-lying pastures of the Becontree and Chafford hundreds there were numerous windmills engaged in milling corn for the London market. At Stratford there grew up a considerable bakery industry, to which there are frequent references in the archives of the City of London. Regrettably, these often record the supply of underweight loaves to the citizenry of the capital. The miscreants found themselves before the court at the Guildhall and were ultimately drawn on a hurdle, with the offending loaves hanging from their necks, to the pillory at Cornhill! Morant, in his history of Essex of 1768, indicates 112 windmills in Essex, including those at Leytonstone, Upminster, Romford, West Ham, Hornchurch, Dagenham and Woodford. This must surely have been an underestimate, for Chapman and André in their survey of 1772 record 187. A century later there were still at least 140 in Essex, but windmills were on the decline in the country generally as the result of the development of electric power. There are perhaps thirty, no more, in Essex today.

The mill at Upminster, to which I shall return, is the pride of Greater London. There were other smock mills at Barking and Mark's Gate, and the latter, Drake's mill, one of the tallest in Essex, was not demolished until 1920 when the structure became dangerous. A post mill stood on Upper Mill Plain at Walthamstow, just by the present site of the Napier Arms, from 1513 to about 1800. There were other post mills at Chadwell Heath and Hornchurch. The Hornchurch mill was working until 1912 but was destroyed by fire, a common hazard with windmills, in 1921. Fire was not the only danger. The machinery, especially the sails, could cause serious injury or even death. A miller, one Jacob Izard, was killed by the rotating sails of the mill at Romford in 1718.

The smock mill, so called because of its supposed resemblance to the traditional working garb of farm labourers, was introduced into England from Holland in the early part of the eighteenth century. The typical and fine example of this type of mill at Upminster was built by James Nokes about 1800, and apart from its obvious aesthetic appeal it incorporates some interesting structural and mechanical features. Thanks to the efforts of the Essex County Council, which acquired it just before World War II, and the

Havering council, which is now responsible for its maintenance, it remains in excellent condition. It mercifully survived being struck by lightning in 1889 and was working until the 1930s, having been in the hands of the Abraham family for three generations. With its handsome deep " petticoat " the mill flaunts its elegant lines, but these do not disguise the sense of power that the giant sails exude. The windshaft on which the sails are mounted was fitted in 1899, having once served a similar purpose in a post mill at Maldon on the Essex coast. The auxiliary steam engine was also secondhand. This was needed to drive the grinding machinery on windless days. The one used at Upminster was from a river boat on the Thames, but was inadvertently destroyed just after the war, during which it had been in safe storage! The sails are carried on a cap shaped like an upturned boat which swivels into the wind through the operation of a fantail. This device, which is automatic, was invented by Edmund Lee. Its vanes are pitched in such a way that it follows a veering wind to hold the main sails square on to it. The four large sails are fitted with remotely controlled chain-operated shutters which can be adjusted according to the strength of the wind. On the cap is a cat-walk used for inspection. This is not often found in English windmills. Around the top of the brick plinth is a gallery from which the sacks of flour and meal were loaded.

There is much more that can be said about the windmill at Upminster, and no visitor to Havering should fail to view it; but first read something about windmills, for apart from enjoying a better appreciation of this fine example windmill literature is worth exploring if only to be introduced to the delightful technical terminology used by the experts. Embedded in esoteric texts one comes across damsels, felloes, shims and warblers—all parts of windmill machinery. I had better leave the subject there lest the remainder of this chapter be neglected.

Here and there, in town and village, will be found an item of great antiquity in the armoury of the law—the stocks. Dating from as early as the Ango-Saxon period, they were widely used in Britain and Europe. Later, in the eighteenth century, they were in frequent use also in the United States, particularly in New England and the southern states.

In England the Statute of Labourers of 1351 required stocks to be erected in every town for the punishment of unruly workers. In 1376 the king, Edward III, was petitioned by the Commons to establish them in every village as a means of dealing with peasant vagrancy. The use of stocks has in fact never been expressly abolished in law, but this degrading aparatus of justice generally died out in the early part of the nineteenth century. There was, however, a case in which they were used in Rugby as late as 1865 and another, for drunkenness in church, at Newbury in 1872. The last recorded instance, at Clifton Hampden in Oxfordshire, with a nice touch of irony, was that in which the village constable was consigned to the stocks for drunkenness and disorderly conduct!

A spell in the stocks was usually the result of relatively trivial offences such as drunkenness, blasphemy and vagrancy, but as well as their use for punishment and correction stocks were available to the village constables for the restraint of offenders while awaiting the arrival of the magistrates. It would seem that things were getting out of hand in Walthamstow in 1645, for the constables formally complained of the lack of this legal convenience in a petition to the justices:

"... in the parish of Walthamstow there is at this present neyther a payer of stockes nor a whipping post, which by the Law ought to be in every parish within this kingdom: the very sight whereof might be a means to keep som from offending the Law, a means for the execution of the Law uppon others: for want whereof the said constables cannot punish offenders. . . . "

In Essex in London the only surviving example still *in situ* that I know of is the eighteenth-century stocks and whipping post on the green by the parish church at Havering-atte-Bower. It was customary to site the stocks on the village green or in some other prominent place, such as the town market. Often they were adjacent to the lock-up and, as at Havering, in convenient proximity to the ducking stool which was available for witches and scolds. Few now remain *in situ*, but the site of the local stocks can often be located on eighteenth-century maps. Sometimes they are to be found in church-yards or even inside churches, to which they have been removed to preserve them, for it would have been considered unseemly to site them on consecrated ground.

Stocks derive their name from the two side posts which support the horizontal boards between which the victims were secured.

Sometimes they were made to accommodate more than one person, and there is even an example at Lyme Regis in Dorset of stocks that would hold four, but that is very rare if not unique. It would be unfair for complacent men of Essex to infer that this reflected the relative needs of the law in the two counties. Stocks on wheels are not uncommon, and it is usually considered that this was to make them portable and thus to facilitate removal to storage when not in use. It has been suggested that stocks were placed on a wheeled platform so that they could be pulled through the town in order to deter potential offenders by drawing attention to this awesome instrument of correction, but this seems highly unlikely, for the conspicuous position which they normally occupied made it unnecessary.

It is always interesting to seek literary references to objects of antiquity, and Shakespeare is an unfailing source. In *The Merry Wives of Windsor* the aggrieved Falstaff complains that " the knave Constable had set me i' the stocks, i' the common stocks for a witch." In more authentic vein, Cornwall, in *King Lear*, after the affray between Kent and Oswald the steward at Gloster's castle, exclaims " Fetch forth the stocks! As I have life and honour, there shall he sit till noon," to which Regan responds with rising enthusiasm for justice " Till noon! Till night, my Lord; and all night too!" Thereupon the offending Kent is put in the stocks for his part in the fracas. A local literary example comes, appropriately, from Tom Hood in his *Tale of the Trumpet* (1841), in which he writes in his familiar brisk style " over the Green and along by the George, past the Stocks and the Church and the Forge." This is a felicitous reference to the village topography of Wanstead in the nineteenth century.

The English landscape, with its intensive patterns of hedged and fenced fields through which common rights of way have been preserved, has made the stile a commonplace object in rural areas. Stiles are found in numerous forms, all designed for the purpose of allowing passage to pedestrians, who must negotiate boundary fences and hedges while denying egress to cattle and other farm animals. In the Greater London area they may be found in parts of the forest boroughs and in the farming areas of Havering to the east.

There was an old distich which asserted:

> " *Essex stiles, Kentish miles and Norfolk wiles*
> *Many a man beguile.*"

The cynics used to hold that Kentish miles only seemed longer because of the state of the roads in that county. In truth I doubt whether they were generally worse than in Essex at one time, and in fact the variation in the Kentish mile was recognized officially in 1633. Some old maps also showed distances in Kentish miles as well as in statute miles. The reference to Norfolk wiles is no doubt an unwarranted reflection on the East Anglian character on which it would be imprudent, not to say indelicate, to speculate, but I am puzzled by the inference that Essex stiles posed greater problems than those elsewhere in England.

Stiles are of great antiquity, references to them occurring in various Anglo-Saxon documents, an early example being in a grant by Offa of *c.* 779. They would therefore merit the attention of some local historian in metropolitan Essex, or in the county for that matter, who might perform an interesting and useful service in recording the types of stile which have been used in the area. They are constructed in a remarkable variety of styles and materials, but the gate type should, strictly speaking, be excluded, for a stile is, taken literally, something to be climbed. The word is derived from the Old English *stigel*, which is itself formed from the verb *stigan*=to climb. It thus has a Teutonic root, the old High German equivalent being *stigilla*. In some parts of northern England and Scotland the word " stile " is also used to indicate a hill, as for example High Stile in the Lake District.

Less conspicuous than the other objects so far mentioned, but no less a symbol of another aspect of our social history, are firemarks, which can be seen by the observant traveller in most of our towns. These attractive little objects relate directly to the development of the fire services and insurance companies and an epic event in the story of the capital.

On Sunday, September 2, 1666, in the early hours of the morning fire broke out in the shop of the king's baker, one Master Farynor, in the City of London. There was nothing unusual about that in the crowded and inaccessible streets of the old city, but on this occasion the fire in Pudding Lane led to one of the greatest conflagrations in history on a scale which Londoners and Thames-side dwellers were not to witness again until the fires of war raged in the city and dockland in 1940. The fire of 1666 burned for over three days and left in the scarred city over 13,000 gutted houses and almost 100 ruined churches.

The great fire had many social and economic consequences. The one with which we are concerned here is the inception and development of fire brigades and fire insurance. The extent of the damage made it imperative that individuals and their businesses should be protected against the irrecoverable losses and ruin that could result from uncontrolled fire. The profound effect which this disaster had on public opinion is demonstrated by the successful establishment of the Fire Office shortly afterwards. The Fire Office was the first in the field to maintain its own brigade and to use fire-marks to identify the properties that were covered by the company's insurance. This indeed was the primary purpose of fire-marks, though they served also to prevent fraudulent claims, since no house was formally covered by insurance until the mark was affixed; nor would the brigades offer any assistance to properties not insured with their parent companies. A secondary purpose was advertisement, and this led to the improvement of design and artistic standards.

It is not known who first conceived the idea of fire-marks, though the City of London once placed a commemorative obelisk on Putney Common to acknowledge this minor contribution to the range of antiquarian objects. The first fire-marks were made of lead and bore the crest of the company and a serial number. The numbers on the lead marks were usually stamped, but there were also rare specimens on which the numbers were embossed. After about 1785 it was found that copper or tinned iron was more suitable and numbering slowly died out. Very rare examples were made in terra-cotta or stone. In Britain the use of fire-plates, as the copper and iron types are called, was discontinued from about 1860, though British companies continued to use them abroad for some years. Hundreds of different designs have been issued by numerous British, American and foreign companies, and some of the insurance companies have large and interesting collections in their city offices.

The first fire-marks issued by the Fire Office have the symbol of a golden phœnix rising from vivid red flames against a dark blue background. The company was later redesignated as the Phoenix Assurance Company and its handsome early marks are collectors' pieces. One amusing and interesting entry in the minutes of the Phœnix records that their messengers were paid twopence for each mark they fixed and were forbidden to solicit gratuities, but continues " he shall ask leave to put up the mark in some conspicuous place and leave the party to their pleasure to pay him for that trouble." Another early company was the Sun Fire Office, whose beaming golden-faced sun is a well-known symbol. It is said that Charles Povey, who introduced the design in 1708, did so from religious motives, but this is not generally accepted and it seems that his acknowledged interest in astronomy was a more likely reason. At all events, the symbol eventually conferred its name on the company, which was not originally so called.

In metropolitan Essex fire-marks may be seen in local museums. The Vestry House museum at Walthamstow, for example, has one in lead dating from 1779, cast as a replica of Britannia and numbered 40532. A corresponding entry in the account books of the overseer of the poor shows that the Vestry House was insured on April 10, 1779, for seven years with the London Assurance Company for a premium of £6/8/6. The Chingford Historical Society, in its museum at Friday Hill House, has a handsome copper fire-plate recovered from a house at King's Head Hill; but it is always more satisfying to see such objects in their original locations, and I am indebted to correspondents of *Essex Countryside* for notes of marks still *in situ* in the area at 39 Hoe Street, Walthamstow, and at 29 Broadway, Rainham. The latter, an eighteenth-century building, is notable for bearing four marks of the Phœnix, Sun and Royal Exchange companies.

Fire-marks are not the only link with the great fire of 1666. Those who know Epping Forest well will be acquainted with the small cast-iron posts, bearing the shield of the Corporation of London, on the roadside by Ambresbury Banks and on Jack's Hill. These two posts are beyond the Greater London limits, but there are others to be found along the old boundary of the Metropolitan Police district where it passed through Havering and Barking and down to the Thames at Dagenham Marsh. Generally they date only from 1851 or 1861, but the history that lies behind these little land-marks is interesting, as I shall briefly relate.

One of the commodities from which the City authorities for long found it expedient and fruitful to raise revenue was coal and another was wine, and no doubt generations of Londoners, not unreasonably, numbered both among the essential creature comforts of life. From the thirteenth century at least a tax was levied on coal, and when, after the great fire, the corporation was left with what at contemporary values was a huge deficit of £240,000 coal readily suggested itself as available for restoring the fortunes of the public purse. Thus in 1667 a duty was levied on coal entering the port of London and a designated area around the capital, ostensibly for the purpose of reconstruction in the city, although it naturally also helped indirectly to service the debt. Further Acts followed at intervals for the next 150 years, and out of its proceeds much was in fact done to promote road schemes and the rebuilding of churches, wharves and prisons. By 1834 the debt had been wholly discharged, but this source of public funds was too lucrative to surrender. The statutory right of the corporation to levy the duties was therefore renewed with the specific object of financing further improvements in London, and many of today's main thoroughfares in the City, such as Queen Victoria Street, St. Martin's-le-Grand and Moorgate, were constructed or improved out of the receipts. The fiscal boundary was at that time at a radius of twenty-five miles from the General Post Office. In 1845 the radius was reduced to twenty miles and in 1861, under the London Coal and Wine Duties Continuance Act, it was again revised to coincide with the Metropolitan Police district. The following year the duties, apart from a metage of four-pence, were transferred to the Metropolitan Board of Works, which, reinforced by the proceeds of these duties, reconstructed the Thames embankments. The board, which was succeeded by the London County Council in 1888, also undertook the drainage and sewerage works, without which nothing could have effectively been done to improve public health in the capital, still subject to recurring and serious epidemics. The Coal Duties Abolition Act of 1889 marked the demise of this ancient source of funds and the last metage was collected in 1890. During the years since the great fire the duties had varied from fourpence to 3/- per ton, and much had been achieved at a time when other sources of local finance for public works were extremely limited.

The posts and obelisks set up under the coal duty Acts varied in size and design. Generally speaking those set up by the canals and the railways were of the larger stone obelisk type up to fifteen feet high, whereas those on the roads were usually between three and four feet high. All bore the shield symbol of the corporation, and normally the date of the Act under which they were erected is indicated, as for example " 24 VICT." In practice relatively little coal was transported on the canals, and it may be wondered why the posts are also sited, as I know to my own discomfort, on inaccessible tracks and certain minor roads. The reason was that coal re-exported from London qualified, when it was taken outside the fiscal area, for a rebate of the duty levied. In Essex in London there were at one time over a dozen posts located along the Metropolitan Police boundary and as many as twenty-seven in Essex on an arc from the Lea to the Thames. Altogether the number of posts around the London boundary totalled some 200 or more. Many of the posts are no longer *in situ*, but apart from the two remaining examples in the forest that I have already mentioned there are others to be seen in the area. One, an obelisk, is by the railway on the old L.N.E.R. route between Chadwell Heath and Romford. Another, of the post type, may be found just inside the Havering boundary at Collier Row. Two more are on the old Dagenham borough boundary and are of some interest in that they still bear the manufacturer's plate. There is also one sited by the entrance to Valence House at Dagenham, having been removed for preservation from its original site in Whalebone Lane.

Coal Duty Post on Jack's Hill, near Theydon Bois

Chapter 6

THE PLACE-NAMES OF ESSEX
IN LONDON

THE scientific and systematic analysis of the origin of place-names in England has made an important contribution to the techniques of modern research and historical interpretation. The work of specialists in this field has thrown new light not merely on local aspects but on general problems such as the pattern and chronology of the settlement of the Anglo-Saxons and the survival of Romano-British communities. If not always conclusive, no local historian can afford to neglect the corroborative evidence that the place-names of his town or village, or of the minor field and geographical features of the district, provide. Thus, aside from the intrinsic fascination of the subject, it is a necessary part of an historical study of any locality to take account of the information which the interpretation of its place-names will yield. But a word of caution: it is essential to start with the earliest known forms of the modern versions and they should be " read " against the background of known historical facts whenever possible.

In Essex most place-names have a Saxon origin, but it is necessary also to watch for assimilated Celtic words as well as for the addition to the Old English vocabulary of names of Scandinavian and Norman provenance. Above all it must be recognized that this is a field for experts and one in which the amateur must trespass with caution. It is certainly ground on which I would not dare to tread without *The Place Names of Essex* and a suitable textbook at my elbow. But there is still scope for the localized study of minor topographical and personal names, though the latter present special difficulty in the London environs of Essex and would be pointless after the middle of the nineteenth century.

Much brilliant scholarship has been lavished on Essex, and Dr. Reaney's erudition is at our disposal in his comprehensive studies of the subject. From these it will be seen that place-names establish conclusively the fundamental Saxon characteristics of the county despite the later periods of Danish and Norman authority. This, as I shall seek to show, is as true of metropolitan Essex as of the county as a whole. It is perhaps convenient first to consider the broad classifications within which place-names can be grouped. Most place-names have some topographical or personal connotation. A name may be derived from the proximity of some conspicuous local geographical feature such as in Leyton, the " village by the Lea," or it may recall the name of a local Anglo-Saxon leader as does Havering (Haeferingas), which denotes " Haefer's people." Indeed, names that end in the derivative " ing(as) " often belong to an important class of place-names in that they usually, though not always, indicate an early Anglo-Saxon settlement, probably of the fifth or early sixth century A.D. This has obvious significance for chronology, but the preceding elements of such names are also of value and it is essential to interpret these from the earliest forms. Place-names ending in " ing " generally denote " the people of " a local leader or " the dwellers at " a particular place, depending on the prefixed element. Among examples in south-west Essex are Barking (Berecingas), meaning " the dwellers by the birch trees "; Roding, " Hrotha's people "; and Epping, " the dwellers on the upland." Most of the " ing " names in Essex occur along the rivers where the Saxons settled before moving on to the clays in the forested areas of the county. Indeed, Saxon Essex is rich in " ing " names, at least twenty-seven being noted as well as some rather later variants in " ingham " and " ington " and with the use of " ing " medially, which at least doubles the total. But most occur in another Saxon county, Sussex, where there are forty-five place-names ending in " ing," and they are fairly numerous too in Kent.

Old English compounds often present problems. Becontree and Wanstead are local examples. The former may be derived from " beacon tree " but is more probably " Beoha's tree," although there is no knowledge of who Beoha was. Wanstead is particularly difficult, but quite likely derives from the Old English Wen Stead, " a place on a hill." Others include Dagenham (" Daecca's home ") and Walthamstow (Wilcumestowe), which either means " a welcome place " or, more probably in my view, is derived from a female personal name.

Names ending in the Old English " ford " are common throughout England. The county town of Essex is a good example, but in metropolitan Essex such names are also frequently found. Ilford,

" the ford over the Hyle," an early name for part of the River Roding, appears in the Domesday survey of 1086 as Ilefort; Woodford is obvious; Romford means " the wide ford "; Chingford, a good example of the necessity of going to an early form (Chaginge-ford), denotes " the ford of the dwellers by the stumps," which is an allusion to the remains of pile dwellings on the Lea. Later, when bridges came to be built in preference to fords, the use of " bridge " in place-names became prevalent. The latest example in our area is Redbridge, which aptly acknowledges the old bridge across the Roding by which Woodford and Ilford were united.

The suffix " tun " invariably refers to a Saxon village and occurs in Leyton, already mentioned, Wennington (" Wynna's tun ") and Upton Park. The last-named is an example of the use of prepositions of place. It appears also in Upminster (" the church on the upland ") and Upney (" upon the marshlands "). In Newham we meet another suffix, " ham," which is difficult. In Higham (Highams Park) and Dagenham it means " home." It can also mean an " enclosure," but in East and West Ham it derives from " hamme," denoting the " flat, low-lying pastures," an accurate description of the Thames-side area before the industrial revolution. In their early forms the two places appear as Estham in 1206 and Westhamma in 1186, but they may be accepted as dating from at least the tenth century. In Rainham we meet an exceptional problem, but philologists believe that its Domesday form, Renaham, may indicate connections with the modern Rainham in Kent, which derives from Roegingas, meaning " a strong people."

At least two names in the area have, or had, the interesting and rare element " atte," which now survives only in Havering-atte-Bower. This is an assimilation of " at the " in an abbreviated form and occurred also in Leytonstone, which was Leyton-atte-Stone in 1370. This, since the stone is connected with the Romans in legend, brings us to two Saxon names in the area inspired by Roman works. The first, Stratford, is not uncommon. In the Old English it is " stret," itself developed from the Latin *strata*, which meant a paved Roman road. It was, of course, at Stratford by Bow that the Roman road to Colchester traversed the Lea. Farther out this road, built primarily for military purposes, has endowed Hare Street (Here Stret) at Romford with its modern name. It means literally " army road," occurs three times in Essex and is also found elsewhere in Britain.

Pre-Roman Britain was Celtic, and I have already suggested that some of our local place-names owe their provenance to these tribal communities. It is true that this is not so with most of our place-names, but Celtic origin should always be suspected, unless there is positive evidence for a later derivation, in river names and those of other natural features. They may also appear as reductions from the names of British tribes or heathen deities. In our rivers, for example, the Thames (Tammasus) itself is Celtic and probably means " dark water." The Lea, too, is probably derived from a Celtic deity, Lugus, or alternatively means " bright river." Do not be deceived by the Beam River at Dagenham, the Ching or the Roding. They are all back-formations, which means that they have in comparatively recent times taken their names from the locality and different early forms are known in each case from documentary evidence. The Ingrebourne is probably formed from the personal name Ine, " bourne " meaning " a stream." If Celtic names are rare in this area those with a Scandinavian etymology are even more so. Snaresbrook is a local example, and a very few others may be found in minor field names such as " holm " on Chingford marsh.

The forest has naturally endowed the area with a number of place-names. Among these are Hainault, meaning " a holt(wood) possessed by the church," in that case Barking abbey, and Ruckholt (Rookwood), not to mention Forest Gate, Woodgrange and Waltham Forest. Other ecclesiastical connotations may be found in Pole Hill (St. Paul's Hill) at Chingford, Abbey mills and Monk's mill at Stratford, which once belonged to the abbey of Stratford Langthorne, and Barley Lane from Dorothy Barley, the last abbess of Barking.

I have already warned of the pitfalls of this fascinating and rewarding aspect of local history. A few convincing local examples of the necessity for caution before accepting apparently obvious interpretations will suffice to illustrate this point. Hawkwood in Epping Forest is nothing to do with those predatory birds, but is derived from Chingford " Halk," meaning " a recess " or " a secluded corner " of the forest. Snakes Lane at Woodford was not the haunt of dangerous reptiles, as we find that in 1404 there lived in the vicinity a John Sake and in 1583 there is Sake's Lane, now picturesquely but inaccurately corrupted by an intrusive " n." Whipp's Cross has no connection with the chastisement of criminals, being a development of Phypp's Cross. But Gallows Corner is authentic, showing that we can sometimes accept a place-name at its face value. Collier Row is orthodox too, and refers to the charcoal burners in the forest, its Middle English version being " Colier." Maryland Point at Stratford was indeed named after the American colony by a successful merchant adventurer. A very recent example of such names is Beckton, named, in 1869, after S. A. Beck, the governor of the Gas Light and Coke Company.

Perhaps the most intriguing names in the area are Seven Kings and Hornchurch. The former appears in a document of 1285 as Sevekyngges. Local tradition suggests that it was the meeting place of seven Saxon kings, and it has even been associated with the heptarchy. This is highly dubious, and Dr. Reaney has suggested the alternative derivation from Seofecingas, meaning " the settlement of Seofeca's people," which would seem more consistent with local history. Hornchurch is as enigmatic as the horned bull's head rebus on the eastern gable of the chancel of St. Andrew's. Its early forms are confusing. *Ecclesia de Haveringis* occurs in 1163 and *monasterum cornatum* (horned monastery) appears in 1222. In 1233 there is Hornechurch in the priory documents and there is Hornedechirche in 1291. By 1493 we have Thornchyrche and in 1604 Herne church. There is some possibility that the name is associated with the bull's head on the seal of the priory in the fourteenth century, but the relationship is nebulous. The rebus does not seem to have been placed on the church before the eighteenth century, though it is possible that there were previously antlers from a deer killed in the locality by, according to a rather weak local tradition, the king's hounds. Another possibility is that the symbol is connected with the tanning industry that was carried on in the medieval village. All in all the name baffles analysis, and possibly the original form, if known, would show that all the " horn " versions derive from an early corruption.

Before closing this chapter it is appropriate to refer briefly to the name of Essex in London itself. We may also call it metropolitan Essex or London over the border. No simple name suggests itself, and none would be wholly satisfactory that did not either explicitly or by inference embrace both the county and the capital. Essex was, of course, the kingdom of the East Saxons and London was its capital. London itself has a Celtic etymology denoted in its Latinized form, Londinium, " Londino's town " being the current favourite of this oft-interpreted name. In the fourth century there was an abortive attempt to change the name of Roman London to Augusta, but, as the capital of Great Britain, the great city bears today an appropriate British appellation.

I hope I have written enough on this cursory survey of the toponomy of the area to encourage the general reader to look farther into this absorbing subject. I hope also to have prompted industrious enthusiasts to compile a complete survey of all place, field and road names in their localities, for there are still many names to record and evaluate despite the masterly and encyclopaedic catalogue in *The Place Names of Essex*.

St Helen & St Giles, Rainham

Chapter 7

THE BOROUGHS

BARKING

Industrial Thames-side

THE whole of Barking's story can be virtually summed up in a few words. The abbey, the fishing industry, Fords and Becontree have been the dominating features of the life and growth of the Essex parishes which were combined to form the Greater London borough in 1965. For the greater part of 900 years the great abbey presided over the area and its various endowments in other parts of Essex and even farther afield. The abbey provided not only social and religious leadership but the stimulus to economic growth. When, after the dissolution of the monasteries, the influence of the abbey was removed it was the fishing industry that raised Barking to national importance as a fishing port and the main supplier of the capital's fish. The hiatus between the demise of the fishing industry and the arrival of Fords on the Thames-side marshes was brief. In the early 1920s the simultaneous development of a vast and dynamic motor-car industry and the then largest housing estate in the world transformed these riverside parishes into the industrial communities of today. Except in tucked-away corners like Dagenham's diminishing village centre it is difficult to escape from the environmental aura shed by the monotonous overgrowth of planned residential areas. But let us first contemplate the stirrings of Anglo-Saxon England from which Barking can date its birth, for Roman and pre-Roman occupation was negligible.

Settlement on the gravel terraces of the low-lying Thames-side levels below the forest line was relatively early in the Anglo-Saxon period and a prosperous farming community was established there by the seventh century, but it was the foundation of the abbey, probably on the land between the Roding and the Back River, that conferred upon Barking a status and influence to which none of the other Anglo-Saxon settlements in south-west Essex could aspire.

One of the greatest and richest of the religious houses of Essex, Barking was founded in the seventh century A.D. and was for many centuries the most powerful nunnery in Britain. Through its great abbesses the abbey exercised a significant influence on the secular as well as the religious life of English society, especially in its earlier phase. It was not until Henry VIII laid his rapacious hands upon it that its glory finally departed. The precise date of its foundation is not known, but January 666 is that usually accepted. In his *History of the English Church and People* the Venerable Bede described the establishment, during Sebbi's reign in the kingdom of Essex, by Eorcenwald, later the Bishop of London, of two famous monasteries, those of Chertsey, over which he himself presided, and Barking, to which he appointed his sister Ethelburga. The abbey was endowed and sustained by the East Saxon nobility, and there is extant a charter, of rare antiquity, issued in 692 by Aethelred confirming the abbey in its lands and privileges. At first the abbey housed both monks and nuns, although it was ruled by an abbess. Later it was established purely as a Benedictine nunnery, its abbesses enjoying precedence over all others. Its royal connections were always close. Soon after its foundation Aethelred transferred forty hides of his land to the abbey as a gift, and for a long period the office of abbess was a royal nomination. Henry I appointed his queen, Maud, to this office, and Stephen's queen, Matilda, was also abbess for a time. During John's reign ecclesiastical dispute led to a reversion to the former practice whereby the nuns elected the abbess, whose appointment then received a formal royal endorsement.

Splendid and powerful as it was, the abbey was not immune from calamity. Periodic flooding was a consequence of the choice of site, and Bede tells of plague at the monastery and of a miraculous vision that preceded the death of Ethelburga. But apart from the dissolution the most disastrous event in the history of the abbey was its destruction by Danish invaders, which is believed, although the period is enveloped in the obscurity of time, to have occurred in 870. According to tradition the abbey buildings were burned down and the monastic community was dispersed. It was not until the tenth century, probably after the reconquest of Essex by Alfred's son, Edward the Elder, or possibly a little later under Athelstan, who ruled from 925-940, that the abbey was refounded. By then restored to its former eminence, the abbey figured in the events surrounding the Norman Conquest. William I established his headquarters there while the great fortress at London was being built on land that had belonged to the abbey. On part of this land now stands the lovely old church of All Hallows-by-the-Tower, its early name, Berkynchirche, acknowledging its early links with the Essex monastery although it was ceded to Rochester cathedral early in the twelfth century.

Despite these vicissitudes the prestige and authority of the abbey continued to increase under the leadership of abbesses who, like Katherine de la Pole and Isabel de Basinges, usually came from the ranks of the nobility or the wealthy classes. During the thirteenth and fourteenth centuries the abbey achieved a dominating position in the life of south-west Essex which it maintained until the dissolution. Barking abbey was not dissolved in the first round of confiscations in 1536, which affected only those foundations, some 200 or so, whose annual income was below £200. But its sun was soon to set, for in 1539 the king's commissioners were received at the abbey, where they had come to effect its surrender to the Crown. The abbess at the time of Barking's demise was Dorothy Barley, who, as chance would have it, was a close friend of Dr. William Petre, as he then was, the court official responsible to the king for the negotiation of the surrender. This poignant coincidence no doubt smoothed the way and ensured that the community received the most advantageous terms that Petre could concede, but it could not affect the main issue. Petre was at Barking to secure its riches for the Crown. Dorothy Barley was obliged to hand over the abbey and all its possessions to William Petre, which she did on November 14, 1539. Oddly enough, the deed of surrender, though bearing the seal of the abbey, was not signed, and it is conjectural as to why this was so. Petre was much too efficient as an administrator to have overlooked this formality. Could it have been that he spared his friend the mortification of that final and painful indignity knowing that it would have no practical consequence in that arbitrary episode? We shall probably never know. Dorothy Barley and the nuns were pensioned and returned to their homes. The demolition of the abbey was commenced soon afterwards, in June 1540, and completed by the end of the following year. At Barking now the only traces of the former magnificence of this great religious house are the curfew tower, which contains the chapel of the Holy Rood, and the foundations, which were excavated in 1911 and reveal the ground plan of the abbey church. The estates were generally alienated from the Crown soon afterwards. William Petre himself purchased abbey lands at Ingatestone, where he built the lovely rose-brick house that graces the slopes below the town today. The manor of Barking and the manorial rights remained in the posterity of the Crown until the reign of Charles I, when they passed to Sir Thomas Fanshawe, the steward of the manor, to whom the land was mortgaged in 1628. The details of this transaction are somewhat obscure, but it is clear that Fanshawe already owned other estates in the vicinity. The subsequent history of the local manors, of which virtually all originated as free tenements of the abbey, is that of descent through various lay families until their ultimate fragmentation.

Nowadays few would think of Barking as a port, but its maritime interests were in fact of cardinal economic importance to the town from the twelfth century. At that time there is evidence of some continental trade, but it was as a fishing port that Barking chiefly developed. The earliest contemporary description we have of the port is that in Defoe's *Tour through the Eastern Counties*. In this narrative he observes that Barking, in 1772, was largely inhabited by fishermen and their families. He also writes of the use of the Barking vessels as " press smacks " which ran to the northern and western ports to pick up seamen to man the fleet, and of their use as auxiliary tenders by the Navy's men-of-war. At that time the Roding was navigable in its lower reaches and the river-based Barking fishermen used to rely on the Billingsgate market, which was already supplying the capital's fish. By the middle of the nineteenth century Barking, as a result of the rapidly expanding demand of the London market, was the most important fishing port in England, and from it operated one of the largest fishing fleets in the world. This situation changed with the advent of refrigeration and the railways, after which the advantage of Barking's proximity to the capital was more than outweighed by its comparative remoteness from the North Sea fishing grounds. The driving force in the development of the Barking fishing fleet from the eighteenth century was provided by the Hewett family. Their Short Blue Fleet, so called from the flag worn by their vessels, pioneered various methods and operating systems to overcome the problems of supplying fresh fish from the Dogger Bank and farther afield. The Hewetts established ice houses supplied from the marshes around Barking, which were artificially flooded in winter to produce ice to be stored to meet the needs of the fish trade through the summer months. They also developed a system of using fast vessels to ferry the catch from the main fleet, which remained at sea, to the Thames—no mean feat of organization. The Barking fleet was already noted for the " well-ships " which were designed to carry live fish in a central compartment in the hull. The level of activity in 1850 may be seen from the fact that some 200 or more vessels manned by some 1,400 fishermen were regularly operating. This naturally fostered the locally based ancillary trades such as rope-making, sail-making, tackle manufacture and shipchandling as well as small shipbuilding. But geography and the development of the capital's railway communications eventually gave the ultimate advantage to the larger-scale enterprises of the east coast ports such as Grimsby, Yarmouth and Gorleston, to which the Barking smacks and most of their crews were transferred. By the end of the century the fishing industry at Barking had come to an end. The Barking smacks, mainly small boats of little more than fifty tons, had pursued their trade as far afield as the Norwegian coast and even in Icelandic waters. Many of the men in the east coast trawler fleets today are the descendants of former Barking fishermen. Two of the local inns at Barking, the Ship and the Ship and Shovel, have names that bear testimony to the industry which, with agriculture, had supported Barking from medieval to Victorian times. The continuity of life in Dagenham, still little more than a rural parish, and Barking was disrupted with the advent of the twentieth century. The former fishing port and the farming community at Dagenham were soon to be usurped by modern industry and the overspill of London's steeply rising population. Fords and Becontree were at hand.

When the two boroughs were combined in 1965 the people of Dagenham and Barking already shared the industrial base on which their economies so largely relied, but throughout much of its history Dagenham had been dominated by Barking, forming as it did part of the abbey domains. In the Domesday survey Dagenham is not mentioned, for it was then part of the episcopal manor. It was only later that the communities of the two parishes developed separately.

Alongside the developing fishing industry at Barking the two parishes formed part of the arable, mixed farming and market-gardening economy of the whole of south-west Essex. By the fourteenth century Barking had already grown beyond the purely rural level of the surrounding communities whose origin and background had been similar. Thus a certain amount of local industry, including tanning, brickmaking, wool and basket making, had been established. This may be attributed entirely to the stimulus of the abbey and Barking's status as a river port. The village straggled between the market place, the abbey environs and the port, and although its population did not rise significantly until the nineteenth century it was about 2,000 by 1801. Dagenham remained a tiny rural settlement concentrated mainly at Becontree Heath and Chadwell Heath. At that time the parish of Barking included Ilford, which was not separated from it for local government purposes until 1888 although the ecclesiastical severance was effected in 1830. During most of that time Dagenham was part of the Romford union and, later, the Romford local board of health for certain local government purposes, one of the first organs of local administration in Dagenham itself being the school board of 1874.

As elsewhere, the advance of population is a useful index of the rate of local economic growth. Although from the middle of the nineteenth century onwards the fishing industry at Barking was declining, new industry was moving into the area, especially on Thames-side and along the Roding. Light engineering, chemicals, cement, woodworking, jute-spinning and manufactured foodstuffs all advanced simultaneously with the population and the development of road and rail communications. By 1850 there were 5,000 people in Barking, but that number was not reached in Dagenham until about 1900. The London-Tilbury-Southend rail route received parliamentary sanction in 1852 and the first section, from Forest Gate to Tilbury, which was routed via Barking and Dagenham, was opened in April 1854, though there was no station at Dagenham on this line until Dagenham Dock was built in 1908. The Barking-Pitsea connection was completed via Upminster in 1888, but again Dagenham, the development of which was still retarded, had to wait until 1895 before the station was built. The only station in the village until then was that at Chadwell Heath, on the line from London to Chelmsford and the east coast, which was erected in 1864.

In Dagenham and to a large extent in Barking the major expansion that took place elsewhere in south-west Essex in the latter part of Victoria's reign was delayed until after World War I. Barking, which had been administered by a local board since 1882, was elevated to urban district status in 1871. This stage of local government was not achieved by Dagenham until 1926. Barking's incorporation as a borough took place in 1931 when the population had reached some 51,000. By then the population of Dagenham, as a result of the development of the Becontree estate by the London County Council to designs and plans produced by its architect, G. Topham Forest, had overtaken that of Barking and had reached about 90,000. Borough status followed in 1938 and the peak population of 115,000 was reached in 1951. At the time of the amalgamation in 1965 the combined population of Barking and Dagenham was about 180,000, the northern tip of Dagenham being included in Redbridge and a small area of Barking in Newham.

Alongside the development of the Becontree estate between 1921 and 1935 there was a remarkable growth of industry in the two towns. Engineering, chemicals, paints, oils and electrical generation all contributed to the expanding industrial base of the economy. Above all there was Fords. Henry Ford's first car—or should one say automobile?—ventured on to American roads in 1896. Although one of the pioneers, Ford was not the first to build a successful car. His achievement was in so transforming manufacturing processes that mass production of what was, and to some extent still is, a luxury article brought motoring within the range of the majority of the population in American and European society. Dagenham has a place in that modern industrial revolution. Ford motor-cars first appeared on the British market in 1903 and by 1912 were being manufactured at Manchester. The expanding market demand led to the establishment of Fords' main plant on the Thames-side marshes at Dagenham. A 500-acre site was purchased in 1925. It was well chosen, for its proximity to a large and growing urban population and the port and communications offered by the river were basic to its success. Henry Ford's son Edsel dug the first sod with a silver spade at the ceremonial opening of the site in 1929. In 1931 Manchester closed and production was commenced at Dagenham. Two thousand employees and their families were transferred to the great manufacturing complex which was rising from the boggy meadows around the Dagenham Breach. The legendary

£100 car was imminent. From then on Dagenham, though still largely a dormitory suburb, was on the industrial map of England. The statistics of this undertaking are astronomical. Tens of millions of pounds have been invested and millions of cars have emerged from the production line at Dagenham. Only a lifetime ago Dagenham was sending modest quantities of potatoes and other vegetables to the London market on horse-drawn carts. Such is the pace and scale of modern industrial enterprise.

Barking, as we have seen, was for centuries familiar with the splendour of its abbey and the royal and important personages which that great foundation attracted. In later times three of the most interesting people with local connections, albeit somewhat tenuous, were James Cook, Elizabeth Fry and Jeremy Bentham. Of Elizabeth Fry, although she lived for a time in a cottage by the Breach and now lies in the Quaker burial ground in North Street, Barking, I shall write in the chapter on Newham, where she spent a significant part of her life; but we may quite properly devote part of Barking's story to the great sailor and the great economist, both of whom seem particularly relevant in the context of Barking's seafaring and industrial traditions.

Some 200 years ago, during the shortening days of August 1768, Lieutenant (later Captain) James Cook sailed from Plymouth in command of the barque *Endeavour* on the first of his great voyages of discovery. He left behind a lonely wife, Elizabeth Batts, of Barking, whom he had married in the parish church of St. Margaret in 1762. The devoted Elizabeth saw all too little of her husband during the eventful years of their married life. It was she who bore the burden of bringing up the three of their six children who survived infancy. It is a pity we do not know more of Elizabeth Batts, for she was clearly a woman of indomitable character who managed to retain her dignity and standards throughout a long life of recurring tragedy. Cook himself, one of the great navigators and hydrographers of British naval tradition, was killed during an affray with natives of Hawaii at Karakokoa Bay in 1779. After this blow Elizabeth suffered the loss of her three sons, who all died within twenty years. Nathaniel and James died at sea and Hugh, only seventeen, at Cambridge in 1780. Mrs. Cook survived her husband by more than half a century, dying at the age of ninety-three on May 13, 1835, and being buried with her sons at St. Andrew the Great, Cambridge. This remarkable Barking lady merits the attention of local historians and a place in any account of the borough's past.

I have seen it erroneously stated that Jeremy Bentham was born in Barking. He was in fact born at Red Lion Street in Houndsditch in 1748, the son of a lawyer, but he certainly had some connections with the Essex village. His work in the field of utilitarian economics had a profound influence on nineteenth-century thought and the political movements of that strident age. This eminent and prodigious writer on political and moral philosophy once wrote, in uncharacteristic vein, that Westminster School was hell, Aldgate was earth and Barking was paradise to him. His nostalgic reflection derived from recollections of boyhood visits to his " aunt Grove " at Barking and the much-admired geraniums at her cottage and the wallflowers sprouting from the crevices in the brickwork of the garden walls.

Pre-eminent among all the buildings of Barking of any age was, of course, the magnificent Benedictine monastic ensemble of which the abbey church formed the dominant feature. In scale it is rivalled by the industrial giant on Thames-side, but spectacular as that undoubtedly is its æsthetic qualities are not obvious. The great abbey church, constructed from the twelfth century, was almost 300 feet in length, with an aisled nave, a tower at the crossing and an apsidal chancel. It was the centrepiece of a fine range of monastic buildings, including a chapter house, a refectory and cloistered precincts. All this is depicted in a reconstruction by Sir Charles Nicholson, in which the superb façades of the great fane and the crowded but ordered outbuildings are seen to dominate the little riverside town. All that is left now lies unobtrusively alongside the parish church. St. Margaret's is a fine Gothic structure built in Kentish rag and ashlar. The chancel dates from the thirteenth century and some elements of the nave are probably earlier. The church also exhibits a number of interesting minor features and well merits the attention of visitors to the abbey site.

The parish church at Dagenham is of medieval foundation, although much of the present fabric dates from the restoration carried out in 1800 by William Mason after the collapse of the tower. In its place he erected an unusual tower which I can only describe as a Gothic travesty, although some have found it impressive, even exciting, despite its weak elevations and curious textures. Nikolaus Pevsner in his description of the building calls it " a true village church in a village street," but in truth it is almost engulfed by extensive residential development and industrial Dagenham. It is not a description that will hold much longer. The dedication of the parish church to St. Peter and St. Paul is one intended, through the association of the names of the two saints, to symbolize Christian unity. Although there are in Essex at least a dozen Anglican churches, nine of which are of pre-Reformation origin, that enjoy that dedication there is only one other, that at Chingford, in Essex in London. The two metropolitan parishes therefore share spiritual as well as geographical and historical affinities with the Anglican communities at Bardfield Saling, Black Notley, Little Horkesley and the other Essex parishes whose churches cherish similar dedications.

Turning now from the ecclesiastical buildings of Barking we must devote a paragraph or so to the two most notable secular buildings of the borough, Valence House and Eastbury House, the architectural merits of which I have acknowledged in another context in this book. Eastbury House was built as a manor house in about 1560 by one Clement Sysley, who purchased the estate in 1556. As I have already remarked, it is a fine example of Tudor architecture, but this is apt to pass without notice, it being better known in local tradition for its alleged association with Lord Monteagle and the Gunpowder Plot of 1605. It has been said that it was at the house, at one time known as Gunpowder House, that the original conspiracy was conceived and that Lord Monteagle was there when he received the letter that revealed the plot. He and the Lord Chancellor consequently surprised Guy Fawkes in the cellars of the parliament buildings, where he was completing the preparations for his intended audacious crime. In fact there is no historical foundation for this unsatisfactory tradition, although it has managed to persist. Barking's only connection with the plot would seem to be that a local sailor and notorious rogue, one Hugh Parish, who ferried Fawkes from the Continent was a Barking man. The house was threatened with demolition in the nineteenth century and again in 1913 when the surrounding estates were developed. It is now leased for welfare purposes to the local authority, but the ownership, and thus the safety, of the building resides in the National Trust.

The pleasantly situated Valence House, now used as administrative offices by the library services and as a Dagenham museum, is the only survivor of the five manor houses in the parish. It derives its name from its fourteenth-century owner Aylmer de Valence, Earl of Pembroke. Once presiding over the largest estate in the parish, the present house, the third on the site, dates from about 1600 and is a charming example of the timbered and plastered buildings of that period. It was originally a moated residence, of which there are still numerous examples in Essex, but the moat has been partly filled in. For many centuries the manor belonged to the deans and canons of Windsor, but locally it is mainly associated with the Bonham and Merttins families. The house was acquired by Dagenham Urban District Council from the London County Council in 1926 and it was used as council offices until 1938. The museum houses a valuable collection of portraits of the Fanshawe family, the owners of the adjacent manor of Parsloes for almost 300 years until the beginning of this century. To a borough in which so few of its secular buildings remain this and Eastbury House are priceless assets.

No topographical study of Barking can neglect the influence that the Thames has exerted on the character and development of the borough. The river has throughout history stimulated the riverine economy of the area and imposed itself physically upon the landscape, sometimes, as in 1707, dramatically and with lasting effect. The Thames-side dwellers have always—even to the present day, as the disaster of 1953 demonstrated—been familiar with the inundation of their lands by the flood tides which occasionally overwhelm the embankments and channels that normally contain them. It is known that the nuns of Barking were forced by the rising waters of the Thames to evacuate the monastic buildings. The vulnerability of the area to the vagaries of the river was again exposed in 1376, when the monks of Stratford Langthorne, now in Newham, transferred to Billericay as a result of extensive flooding. In 1621 a sluice gate was constructed at a particularly vulnerable point by a Dutch engineer, Cornelius Vermuyden, but the defences finally yielded to the inexorable pressure of the flood tide in 1707, when the so-called Dagenham Breach was opened up. On that occasion hundreds of acres of the Dagenham levels and farther west were submerged by the inrush of water after the collapse of the sluices. The speed and scale of the tidal assault appear to have stupefied the authorities, for the efforts made to contain the flood were late and largely ineffective. The advancing waters even reached Dagenham village, and before the end of the year more than 1,000 acres had been engulfed. Inefficient and unco-ordinated measures, including the construction of revetments with piled rubble and soil, the sinking of ballasted hulks and the digging of relief channels, failed to resolve the problem. By 1714 the defences were still insecure and navigation of the river had been seriously impeded by the accumulation of silt and the disintegration of the embankments. The matter was raised in the House of Commons, and in that year was enacted " an Act for the speedy and effectual Preserving of the Navigation of the River of Thames by stopping the Breach in the Levels of Havering and Dagenham in the County of Essex and for ascertaining the Coal Measure." Public parsimony delayed the final solution. A tender from a Mr. Boswell for £19,000, later reduced to £16,500, was preferred to that of a Gloucestershire man, Captain Perry, who had estimated the work at £24,000. After several abortive attempts Boswell conceded defeat and Perry literally stepped into the breach! The result was a landmark in the engineering history of the river. Despite a setback in 1718 when the defences were again breached, financial difficulty and much public controversy Perry finally succeeded and this work stood the test of time. Defoe, who visited the area eight years later, " saw the famous breach " made by the inundation, which, with journalistic exaggeration, he asserts had extended over some 5,000 acres and was by then " effectually blocked." But poor Perry, despite a final contribution from public funds of £40,000, still suffered a financial loss by the time the work was completed in 1720. The area now occupied by the Breach and known as the Gulf is no more than thirty or so acres and is a much-favoured fishing resort. Breach House, demolished in 1812, became famous as the venue of an annual " whitebait dinner," which was attended on the first occasion by William Pitt and afterwards by other members of the Cabinet for many years. This event was later transferred to Greenwich but was finally abandoned about 1880. Today the Dagenham

Breach has itself been engulfed by the modern industry that now dominates the topography of the area.

Sandwiched between this industrial jungle on Thames-side and the residential acres of Becontree is the dwindling though tenacious remnant of Dagenham's village. As I write it comprises little more than the parish church, the eighteenth-century vicarage, the Cross Keys and a few scattered cottages, but the traffic systems are making inroads into what remains and soon only church, vicarage and inn will be left. The somewhat overgrown, but colourful and gay, front gardens of humble cottages provide an informal context for the rather contrived restorations of the parish church and the Cross Keys, and their antiquity will be even further disguised when the cottages make way for modern roadways. The Cross Keys inn, nestling within the lee of the church, is indeed a fine timbered and gabled fifteenth-century house of open hall type. It became an inn towards the end of the seventeenth century, being then known as the Queen's Head. Its later designation as the Cross Keys is clearly inspired from the symbol of St. Peter, which serves to emphasize the association of the oldest secular building in Dagenham with the ancient parish church. Before it assumed its public role it was the home of a tanner, William Comyns, whose family was to achieve social status when in after years his grandson John, whose portrait is in Valence House, acquired a judgeship and a knighthood. Apart from their home in the village the family remain in Dagenham's past associations through a charitable trust which originated, for the benefit of poor widows of the parish, from a land transaction with the Fanshawes. Thus it is that Comyns Cottages derive their name.

The subject of local charities, of which the Comyns Trust was an example, is not without interest. Numerous petty and sometimes eccentric parochial charities, many persisting into recent years, often cast an amusing sidelight on contemporary social attitudes, but they are the bane of administrators and the Charity Commissioners have encouraged local authorities to review and rationalize them in co-operation with trustees so that the full benefit of their revenues can be realized. The local annals of Barking provide a number of prime examples of such bequests. One charity provided for the allowance of a florin to twenty-seven poor fishermen or their dependants. It seems doubtful, to say the least, whether such a number of appropriate recipients could be found in the parish today.

Another allowed for £6/13/4 from the tithes of the rectory of Ash in Kent to be alloted to the relief of the poor of that parish with the exception of the odd 13/4, which could be claimed by the vicar of Barking provided he preached a prescribed sermon. A third, dating from 1556, provided for the supply of charcoal to the poor of Barking at Christmas. Almost all of the local parishes reveal in their records similar examples of quaint and anachronistic charities, but it now seems that their days are numbered.

Historically the heart of the new borough of Barking is perhaps Becontree Heath, for here, it is believed, was the meeting place of the Becontree hundred, the earliest forerunner of today's council. As such it became the focal point of the local road system and an area of settlement. Today it is overrun by modern redevelopment but remains, appropriately, the site of the civic centre, which dates from the 1930s. The pretentious and basically horizontal elevations of the municipal building are today challenged by the verticality of the residential tower blocks now rising, in the modern idiom, high above the old heath. Largely submerged beneath a sea of concrete and tarmac, the heath is now little more than a name, but it epitomizes the continuity of local institutions as the hub of a vast and generally monotonous classless locality, although it is relieved here and there by desultory attempts at vernacular architecture in the Essex style. But, to be fair, Becontree was a social adventure and when it was first developed offered to thousands of Londoners an escape from the slumdom into which they had been born. It may be dull, but it has made a reality of homes in which family life can be lived in security, comfort and dignity. These are no mean criteria.

The riverside areas of the borough contrast dramatically with the residential area to the north. Industrial installations dominate the horizons and sprawl in ugly and chaotic patterns over the former marshlands, which from time immemorial had been worked by Essex farming folk. Along the grassy banks of the humble Beam River there remains a narrow belt characteristic of the meadowland of the old levels. It is hard now to visualize the splendour of the abbey and the tranquillity of the agricultural past of the borough. Perhaps one should not try, for Barking's future is committed to its industrial and urban role.

HAVERING

The royal liberty

OF all the Greater London boroughs of Essex Havering is the most diverse and in many ways the most interesting. It is also the largest, covering an area almost equal to that of Redbridge, Newham and Barking together. Of all the London boroughs only Bromley is greater in extent, but of population Havering has rather less than most and in density it is exceeded by all except Bromley.

The name which was given to the combined borough of Romford and the urban district of Hornchurch is one of great antiquity, with a pre-Conquest derivation. Although at the time of the amalgamation the name of Havering was attached only to the small parish in the north of Romford it in fact recalls the ancient royal liberty, a status unique in the annals of metropolitan Essex, which existed for almost 500 years. The manor of Havering was Crown demesne and was included within the hundred of Becontree, which covered most of the area now comprised within the other London boroughs of Essex. The liberty was roughly that area of the new borough of Havering to the west of the Ingrebourne river. A favoured place of royal residence from Saxon times onwards, Havering was granted various privileges by royal grace and these were incorporated in a charter of Edward IV in 1465 which recognized the area as a royal liberty. The rights enjoyed by the inhabitants of the liberty included toll-free access to roads, bridges, fairs and markets and the maintenance of courts and other institutions of local administration. The charter was confirmed and extended on a number of occasions between the fifteenth and seventeenth centuries, the last being by Charles II in 1664. Romford served as the administrative capital of the liberty, though its parish church was at Hornchurch. In the course of time the organs of government within the liberty, which was sold by the Crown in 1828, and the special privileges of its inhabitants became anachronistic and they were abolished as a result of local-government changes at the end of the nineteenth century. Thus, although the liberty was formally extinguished by Order in Council in 1892, it was a remarkable and happy coincidence that the name of Havering should have been reinstated in 1965, exactly 500 years after the grant of the royal charter. It was fitting too that the royal blue and gold coat of arms should bear the single word " Liberty " as the chosen motto of the new borough. On the shield is superimposed a ring set with a ruby, which recalls the legend that I have retold in writing of the forest earlier in this book. The legend is at least as old as the liberty, for it was recorded in the thirteenth century by Robert of Gloucester. It is a charming story, but unhappily the legends of Havering, unlike those of Waltham Forest, place too great a strain upon credulity.

The first step away from vestry and liberty government towards modern institutions was made in Romford in 1819 when commissioners for paving and lighting were appointed. At that time the population of the parish was only a few thousand and had not increased significantly when the local board of health was established in 1852. In Hornchurch development was even slower, and there, as in the remainder of what is now Havering, parish government continued throughout the nineteenth century. But the area was inevitably involved in the general development that followed the railways in south-west Essex, although the tempo was noticeably slower than in the districts nearer to London. Romford became an urban district in 1895, when there were about 12,000 inhabitants. This stage was not achieved in Hornchurch until a comparable level of population was reached in 1926. In 1901 part of the Romford rural area was included in the urban district and much later, in 1934, Havering-atte-Bower and Noak Hill were also added. A similar process took place at Hornchurch when, by the Essex Review Order of 1934, Upminster, Cranham, Rainham and part of Great Warley were transferred to it from the Romford rural district. North Ockendon was transferred from the Orsett rural district in 1936. By then Romford was ripe for borough status, which was conferred in 1937. Hornchurch never became a borough, although by 1965 its population, at around 35,000, was rather larger than that of Romford.

It is not easy to decide where to begin an account of this large and varied borough, but it might be thought appropriate to leave aside the main centres of population at Romford, Hornchurch and Upminster for a moment and look first to the relatively unimportant but historic Havering-atte-Bower. This village, for it is hardly more, is located in the parklands to the north of the borough. Here were

the country homes of the kings and queens of England from Edward
the Confessor to Charles I, but its former glory has departed and it
requires an effort of the imagination to recall the scenes of regal
splendour that were enacted in this now pleasant but unassuming
quarter of the old liberty. The motto of the former urban district
of Hornchurch, " A good name endureth," was nevertheless ful-
filled in an unexpected way when the name of this small village was
conferred on it as well as Romford in 1965, thus restoring " Havering " to its former prominence in this part of Essex.

There were two royal residences at Havering-atte-Bower. One was
situated close by the site of the present parish church to the south-
west of the village green; the other, Pyrgo, lay about a mile north-
east of the village in gracious parkland. The palace at Havering-
atte-Bower was a much favoured retreat of Edward the Confessor,
from whom the royal manor passed to Harold. Another of Havering's improbable legends holds that the nightingales never sang
during the Confessor's sojourns there, in order that the saintly
monarch's prayers should not be disturbed! After Harold's death
at Hastings the manor was confiscated by the Crown. The palace
was particularly associated with English queens. Following its
grant, in 1267, by Henry III to his wife, Eleanor of Provence, it
came to be regarded as a dower house, though it also served the useful purpose of keeping controversial royal ladies out of the political
limelight. Richard II, son of the Black Prince, came to the throne
in 1377 in difficult circumstances. His reign was overlaid with social
and dynastic dispute which eventually led to his deposition. His
second marriage, to Isabella, the daughter of the French king, took
place in 1396 when she was only seven; but when three years later
John of Gaunt's son assumed the throne as Henry IV Isabella was
taken into custody and lodged in turn at Sonning in Berkshire and
at Havering-atte-Bower. Subsequently, in 1401, her return to France
was negotiated, but the ill-starred child, by then married to the Duke
of Orleans, died in 1409 at the early age of twenty. The absolute
monarchy of Richard II was followed by the dynastic and constitutional uncertainties of the reign of Henry IV. Joanna of Navarre,
his second wife, also has a place in the story of Havering-atte-
Bower, for after Henry's death in 1413 she retired to Pyrgo, which
had formed part of her jointure when she became queen. It was
there that she died in 1437 amid accusations of indulgence in witchcraft. The charges were false and it is probable that they were in-

spired by mercenary motives, since the finances of the Crown had
sunk dangerously low as a result of rising expenditure occasioned
by the French wars. The allegations of witchcraft would therefore
have constituted a plausible reason for the confiscation of the queen's
dowry for the benefit of the state revenues. Curiously, Henry's life
had also ended in circumstances significant to the superstitious attitudes of the fifteenth century, for in fulfilment of a premonition
that he would die in the Holy City he expired in the Jerusalem
chamber of Westminster Abbey after collapsing while at prayer.

The heyday of Havering's associations with the English queens
was still to come, however. The boy king Edward VI, Mary Tudor
and Elizabeth I were all lodged there as children, discreetly absent
from the political life of the capital. Among the features of Elizabeth's reign were the triumphant " progresses " she made throughout the country. A number were made in Essex and usually started
from Havering-atte-Bower. The first progress made in the county
took place in 1561, just three years after the queen's accession.
Others followed in 1568, 1571, 1578 and 1579. During the progress
of 1568 Elizabeth was entertained at Gidea Hall, Romford, the
house of Sir Anthony Cooke, to whom I shall recur. The Elizabethan progresses were carried out on a grand scale and, as they
were intended, did much to enhance the queen's personal popularity. She enjoyed the adulation of Londoners, who saw much of
her, but in the counties too she was received with loyal acclamation
and lavish hospitality wherever she went. Elizabeth courted her
people with the same art and consummate skill with which she pursued her political policies. She never lost her appetite for what
journalists would today describe as " whistle-stop tours." So that
the people could see her better the queen frequently rode quite a
long distance on horseback or in an open carriage. As the royal
procession reached the county boundary there would be speeches
from the local dignitaries, presentations, fireworks, and even gun
salutes. The rapturous receptions with which she was greeted in
1568 were described by the Spanish ambassador in such terms as
to leave no doubt in the minds of his government of Elizabeth's
personal position. The queen was also at Havering-atte-Bower
during the approach of the Armada in 1588, and it was from there
that she went to Tilbury to deliver her memorable speech " Let
tyrants fear . . . " to Leicester's troops as they awaited the assault
of the enemy forces then massed under Parma on the Continent.

After Elizabeth's death Havering's age of royal favour was soon to draw to a close. The dour and pedantic James I was more attracted to Theobalds and Wanstead, and the royal residence at Havering-atte-Bower was allowed to fall into disrepair. Charles I was the last of the English monarchs to stay there. He did so on the occasion of his meeting at Moulsham Hall, Chelmsford, in November 1638 with his mother-in-law, Marie de Medici, the queen mother of France, who was then visiting England to see her daughter Henrietta Maria. That night the queen mother slept at Gidea Hall, Romford, while Charles and his entourage stayed at Havering-atte-Bower. A contemporary print, of admittedly doubtful authenticity, shows the splendid procession of coaches, heralds and outriders assembling at " Gidde Hall " for the departure to London the next morning. In 1652 the palace was sold to Richard Deane, one of the judges who had signed the warrant for Charles's execution. After the Restoration desultory efforts were made to keep the residence in repair, but it was fast becoming a ruin and by the early nineteenth century it had completely disappeared and the estate had been fragmented. Pyrgo was dismantled in 1770.

Indirectly associated with the royal residence is the Bower House, for materials from the ruined palace were used in constructing the foundations for it. This attractive brick-fronted house appeals to all tastes. It dates from 1729, when it was built for John Baynes, serjeant at law, " that he might retire into sure ease and have pleasant leisure for himself and his friends." The architect was Henry Flitcroft, the Bower House being his first major work. Like many of the leading architects of his day, including Kent, Flitcroft was a craftsman before he turned to architecture. The son of one of William III's gardeners, he was trained as a joiner. Later he became one of Lord Burlington's draughtsmen and protégés, earning the sobriquet of " Burlington Harry." His best known work in London is St. Giles-in-the-Fields. He also built Woburn Abbey for the Duke of Bedford and Wentworth Woodhouse, the latter being the largest house in England. The Bower House is not to be compared with such imposing work, but it is none the less an adornment to the pleasant environment of this corner of Havering. The house is now owned by the Ford Motor Company, which uses it as a training centre, and thus it is maintained in excellent condition. Occasionally the company allows access to the public, and this provides an opportunity to see the interior, which is notable for a

splendid fireplace and Thornhill's wall painting on the main staircase. The house has not been the scene of great events, though it
was visited by Princess Charlotte in 1801 and Queen Mary in 1934,
thus enlarging Havering's traditional associations with England's
royal ladies. Perhaps the most noteworthy event in the story of the
house was the feast held there in 1832 to celebrate the enactment of
the Reform Bill, when the poor of the village were entertained. It
is reasonable to assume that most of the guests were more impressed by the fare than by the franchise, if only because they were
the recipients of the one but not the other!

If Havering-atte-Bower is the spiritual heart of Havering borough
Romford is its centre of gravity. There the market place symbolizes
the importance of the town to the whole of this part of Essex.
Developing from Oldchurch and the crossing at the Rom, settlement stretched eastwards until by the end of the fourteenth century
the village was focused around the market place. Here was established a flourishing country market trading in sheep, cattle and
agricultural products as well as leathers and skins from the pelt
merchants of neighbouring Hornchurch. Its origins are obscure,
although it was chartered by Henry III in 1247. However, thirteenth-
century charters did not of themselves normally confer privileges;
they usually constituted no more than formal confirmations of
existing franchises. It was only later that they came to be regarded
as a source of rights and privileges. We cannot therefore establish
with any certainty the date of the market's foundation, but it is, by
the evidence of the charter, of great antiquity. In 1636 John Taylor,
who called himself the "king's water poet," though he is disparagingly
described as " a literary bargee " in the *Dictionary of National
Biography*, made a pleasant reference to the Romford market in
one of his numerous works. In compiling a list of Essex inns, in
which he included the Angel, the Bell, the White Hart and the Cock
at Romford, he wrote of " a sweet, savery, clean and gainful market
for Hoggs." An attractive eighteenth-century print shows the market
place, brooded over by the square battlemented tower of old St.
Edward's, to be a lively concourse of cattle, sheep and visitors milling around the spacious trading centre of this growing community.
When the liberty was sold by the Crown to Hugh McIntosh in 1828

all its rights, including that of holding the market, were transferred to his ownership. It remained in his posterity until 1892, when the family were in dispute with the local board and following their refusal to carry out certain improvements the market was closed by order of the Board of Agriculture. The result of this confrontation was the acquisition of the market by the local authority, which has maintained it ever since. It is still a thriving institution and is thronged on market days with a surging congregation of shoppers who come from a wide area in search of bargains, but cattle have not been marketed there since 1958.

One of the best local buildings at the upper end of the market place is the Romford charity school. This school was founded by Joseph Bosworth in 1710 and accepted poor children from Havering-atte-Bower and Hornchurch as well as Romford. The agreeable old red-brick building was erected in 1727 and continued as a school until 1926, although it had been combined with the new National school in about 1835. After 1926 it was taken over as a public library and served this purpose until the recent construction of the fine modern central library in Laurie Square. The extensive redevelopment planned for the town centre of Romford may well involve the demolition of this old building, so at the time of writing its days seem to be limited. While on the subject of Laurie Square it is perhaps worth mentioning that Laurie Hall was built on the site of the old Loam Pond after it had been filled in about 1874. This building, appropriately used as a county court, thus stood upon the place where the village stocks and other instruments of correction were sited in the market place. Nearby Ducking Stool Court is an apt reminder of those sterner times. Another sidelight on the social organization of eighteenth-century Romford is afforded by the rules of the local workhouse made by the directors and guardians of the poor in 1787. These rules date from the period of the Gilbert Act of 1782, which marked the reversal of the traditional concept of poor-law administration. An Act of 1601 had placed upon the parish authorities, which were often unable to bear it, the obligation of providing suitable work for the poor in return for their subsistence. The Act of 1723 permitted the maintenance of workhouses for this purpose and relief was withheld from those who refused to enter them. Thomas Gilbert's Act broadened the basis of administration and provided for relief or work outside the workhouses, which were reserved for all classes of the destitute except the able-bodied. The Romford rules, which reflect the growth of humanitarian influences in the eighteenth century, direct the master to register the poor, keep regular accounts, read daily prayers, supervise the meals and " see that the paupers sit decently." The mistress of the house is to see that the rooms are swept and cleaned and " the dishes, platters, trenchers, bowls and piggins " washed twice daily. She must also see that the children are washed and groomed, taught to read and catechized twice a week. Both are to take care to see that the apothecary attends the sick and lame.

Apart from its comparatively obscure but significant role in the life of Romford the market place has witnessed events that command a minor niche in national history from the time when the Roman legions first traversed the route from Londinium to the colonia at Colchester. Saxon and Norman invaders, king's men and rebels, cavaliers and roundheads have all trodden the same path. Nearer our times, in 1761, the Princess Charlotte of Mecklenburg took coffee at the Queen's House in the High Street. Here she was met by the royal coach and escort to be taken to the capital for her marriage to the reluctant George III. Shortly afterwards, in 1768, there was born the second daughter of the Duke of Brunswick and the Princess Augusta. The infant was destined to become the controversial and ill-used queen of George IV of England. Princess Caroline of Brunswick-Wolfenbüttel married George, then prince regent, in 1795 and his sordid conduct aroused considerable public sympathy for the unhappy queen. There were unseemly scenes at George's coronation in 1821 when the queen was refused access to the abbey. She died in the following month. In Essex there was passionate feeling about Caroline, and the hearse, *en route* for Harwich and the Continent, was escorted by excited crowds. After an affray at Hyde Park Corner, in which life was lost, the dismal procession reached Romford during the afternoon and the cortège rested in the market place. There, despite torrential rain, a large crowd of sympathizers had collected, and when the journey was resumed later that night the procession was preceded by local torchbearers. At Colchester there were further demonstrations by rival factions in which some of the leading Whigs in the county were implicated. Caroline was eventually laid to rest in the royal vault at Brunswick on August 26, 1821. Thus ended another episode of Havering's numerous, but usually happier, associations with the monarchy.

Prominent in Havering's gallery of worthies was Francis Quarles the poet, who was born at the manor house of Stewards at Romford in 1592. After graduating from Christ's College, Cambridge, in 1608 he studied law at Lincoln's Inn but later turned to literature. A prolific writer of religious and meditative prose and poetry, his reputation was established by the publication in 1635 of " Emblems," which he wrote at Roxwell in Essex. He was married in 1618 to Ursula Woodgate and they had eighteen children. In politics, although he had a puritan background, he supported the royalist cause and wrote a number of pamphlets opposing the parliamentarians. The latter years of his life were dogged by poverty, but he received some support from the influential Barrington family of Essex and secured the post of chronologer to London in 1640. Harried by the parliamentarians, he died in 1644 and was buried in the City of London at St. Olave's. There is a painting of Quarles by William Dobson in the National Portrait Galley. Quarles's work does not appeal to modern taste, but his posthumous popularity was such that many of his numerous works were frequently re-printed for over a century after his death. It was once even said— I cannot remember by whom and on this point my notes fail me— that " Milton was forced to wait until the world had done admiring Quarles." That his name could be coupled with Milton at all is testimony enough to the contemporary appeal of the curious mix-ture of native wit, piety, fervour and melancholia in his writings.

In Romford too lived Humphry Repton, whom I have already introduced, but a word about the man, rather than about his work, would be apposite here. This celebrated landscape gardener lived and practised at the Hare Street district of Romford for about thirty years. An East Anglian, born at Bury St. Edmunds in 1752, he at first associated with Lancelot (Capability) Brown, his eminent contemporary, but eventually developed his own more varied style. Repton carried out a certain amount of work in Essex, including the grounds at Highams and Hill Hall. He also practised widely in the southern counties and London, and Russell Square, Blooms-bury, was laid out to his design. He lived in a cottage at the junction of Balgores Lane and Main Road until his death in 1818.

Another of the great men of Romford was the learned Sir Anthony Cooke, whose remarkable family, recovered from its misfortunes during the Wars of the Roses, was prominent in Romford for nearly two centuries, during which it resided at Gidea Hall. Tutor to

Edward VI, Cooke brought up his family in an atmosphere of scholarship, but he is often remembered for the advantageous marriages that his equally talented daughters contracted. One, Mildred, espoused Lord Burleigh; Elizabeth married Lord Russell and Katherine Sir Henry Killigrew; a fourth, Ann, became the second wife of Sir Nicholas Bacon, Lord Keeper of the Great Seal of England. To this last-named union was born at York House in the Strand a son, Francis, to whom some attribute the works of William Shakespeare. Notwithstanding the slight possibility that Bacon was the true author of some of Shakespeare's work, his literary and political eminence is fully established and Romford may claim a connection with this famous man through Anne Cooke. Sir Anthony, who was steward of the liberty of Havering, is commemorated by a fine memorial transferred to St. Edward's from the old parish church. He is depicted in Tudor armour and his wife is dressed in a gown and ruff of the period. Their two sons and four daughters are also included in the group. The Latin epitaph is reputed to have been composed by one of the daughters of this erudite family.

I have referred earlier to the Essex connections with the Gunpowder Plot of 1605 in writing of Lord Monteagle and Eastbury House in Barking. A lesser known citizen of Romford was one John Babington, who greatly preoccupied himself with the subject of fireworks, with which we now associate this infamous episode. His name is preserved in one of the minor roads of Romford, though it is doubtful whether anyone in the town these days associates it with this obscure, if spectacular, science. Born in 1604, Babington, a mathematician and an artillery expert, published in 1635 a work entitled *Pyrotechnica, or a Discourse of Artificiall Fireworks*. At about this time tacticians were beginning to exploit the military possibilities of pyrotechnics, and Babington's book was concerned with this aspect of the subject as well as with the more familiar purposes. In dedicating his book to the Earl of Newport, Master of the King's Ordnance, Babington described himself modestly as " one of the inferior gunners of his Majestie." He also produced work on geometry and logarithmic tables for gunnery. He died in 1645. His only known portrait, by Droeshout, is at Chatsworth.

★   ★   ★   ★

From bustling Romford we turn now to the gentler aspect of Hornchurch, which has grown up alongside the Ingrebourne. It is here that one senses the loosening grip of the metropolis upon the Essex boroughs. The town's most conspicuous landmark is the soaring spire of the lovely parish church of St. Andrew on its dominating site that commands the slopes which drop away on either side of the two rivers of Havering. I have dealt in some detail in an earlier chapter with the enigma of the name of Hornchurch. Suffice it to say here that among the less probable theories of the origin of the name is that it derives from the horns of a hart killed by the king's hounds near the church at the time it was under construction, the horns being subsequently placed on the nave wall. There is still a rebus in the form of a bull's head at the top of the gable above the east window. Carved from the stone and embellished with copper-covered horns, the present head dates from the eighteenth century, though it was no doubt a replacement for an earlier version. The most likely explanation of the rebus is that the horns were placed on the church to symbolize the staple industry of the area and to associate it in that way with the parish church. Main Road in Hornchurch was once called Pelt or Pell Street on account of the concentration of skinners, tanners and other leather trade workers who carried on their businesses there for perhaps 600 years until towards the middle of Victoria's century.

Hornchurch was notable in the past not only for leather goods but as a sporting venue, particularly at the Millfield, or the Dell, just behind the parish church. This field was the scene of cock-fighting, wrestling and prizefighting in the eighteenth century. The most famous contest to be held there was that between the pugilists Mendoza the Jew and Jackson which took place in 1795 for a stake of 200 guineas. A large crowd of several thousands, including the "quality," such as the Duke of Hamilton and Lord Delaval, saw Jackson win in the ninth round. Havering is still host to Essex cricket in most seasons, as the county side now plays several of its fixtures at Romford, but the borough's cricket tradition really rests on the enthusiasm and prowess of the men of Hornchurch, who played many a famous match at Langtons from the foundation of the club in 1783 until well on into the next century. In 1830 they defeated " all Essex " in a match sponsored by Tom Rounding, whom we have already met, at Woodford Wells. In 1831 they had the temerity to hold the M.C.C. to a draw at Lord's. Although the return match at Langtons was lost it had been a brave performance on the part of the village side. In 1834 they defeated Chelmsford,

West Essex and Ingatestone. In any event, win, lose or draw there was solace to be had at the Bull inn or the White Hart, to which the teams customarily retired after stumps were drawn.

One of the sporting traditions of Hornchurch was the wrestling tournament held on the Millfield each Christmas Day. The reward for victory in this annual contest was a boar's head, which with due ceremony was presented by New College, Oxford, which was connected with Hornchurch through William of Wykeham, its founder. William of Wykeham was a remarkable man. He first entered the service of the State as king's clerk and his energy and ability carried him via the rectorship of Pulham in Norfolk to his appointment as canon and prebend at Lichfield in 1359 and ultimately his enthronement as Bishop of Winchester in 1368 and the Chancellorship of England. But he incurred the enmity of John of Gaunt, then a power in the land, who in 1371 inspired his impeachment by the House of Commons for the misapplication of revenues and other alleged illegal activities. In the event he was condemned on only one relatively minor count and following the death of Edward III was pardoned. In the course of his brilliant career William of Wykeham amassed a very considerable fortune, some of which he deployed in support of his new foundations of Winchester College and New College at Oxford. It was thus that he came to purchase former monastic property at Hornchurch, which included the church and the manors of Suttons and Newbury in Havering as well as associated property in London. The history of this property is interesting and has a possible bearing on the name of Hornchurch, for the " horned monastery " (*monasterium cornatum*) was that established at Hornchurch in 1158 on land granted by Henry II to the monastery of St. Nicholas and St. Bernard at Montjoux in Savoy. Before the end of the fourteenth century the affairs of the priory were in serious decline and there was local hostility towards this foreign foundation when it was confiscated by the king and alienated in turn in 1391 to William of Wykeham, who granted it as part of his endowment of New College.

Thus are St. Andrew's and Hornchurch associated with this famous man. The church is also the resting place of another servant of the state, Thomas Witherings, who, if somewhat mundane by comparison, is none the less worthy of his place in the story of Hornchurch. This competent and industrious man, who lived at Nelmes, was a pioneer of postal reform. Serving as postmaster of England in Charles I's administration, he modernized the limited and inefficient services that had grown up haphazardly in the Tudor and early Stuart periods. Under his direction mails were speeded up and the operations of the service extended. He also devised systems of postmarking and registration and vigorously pursued the policy of a self-supporting service, a concept that has a modern flavour. In fact the methods and principles he introduced remained as the basis of postal administration until the reforms of Rowland Hill in the nineteenth century. But his administration was chequered with parliamentary and legal controversy and he died a harassed man in 1651, reputedly on his way to a service in St. Andrew's, where he is buried. His epitaph, too long to quote in full, is worthy of note: " Chief Postmaster of Greate Britaine and foreign parts, second to none for unfathomed policy, unparalleled, sagacious and divining genius. . . . "

We shall now cross the modest Ingrebourne to Upminster and the mainly rural districts of Essex in London. Here we are in the marginal lands of the borough, and many would argue that this little river would have been a more logical boundary with the county than the somewhat arbitrary bounds of the outlying parishes. Upminster is certainly still a town with its own identity despite the development of recent decades which has merged it with the Romford-Hornchurch urban complex. Its most conspicuous landmark is, I suppose, the magnificent windmill in St. Mary's Lane which I have happily lingered over in another chapter. Let any quixotic developer tilt at this one who dares.

The windmill is but one of Upminster's splendid range of surviving buildings in the county's traditional medium of timber. Upminster Hall at the golf course is a fine example. Close by is the superb timber-framed tithe barn, an outstanding building of its kind. Great Tomkins completes a group of rare quality. The parish church, farther south, although now largely a product of Victorian restoration, still possesses its robust thirteenth-century timber-framed tower, which is of an unmistakable Essex vintage. Upminster is a good place in which to savour the craftsmanship of Essex carpenters. It is also a place to contemplate those Essex scholars the fertility of whose inventive minds, like that of Derham, who was rector here for over thirty years, contributed so handsomely to the incipient science of modern times.

In reviewing the contribution made in Essex to the physical sciences we think first, I venture to suggest, of William Gilberd, of Colchester, and his work on magnetism in the sixteenth century, and of Crompton and Marconi, who pioneered electrical engineering and telegraphs at Chelmsford. Essex in London is represented in this distinguished company by William Derham, the versatile rector of Upminster. He was born at Stoughton, near Worcester, on November 26, 1657, and educated at Trinity College, Oxford. Later he became a leading member of a group within the Royal Society which included such eminent men as Newton, Wren and Ray. In 1689 he was appointed to Upminster and married a Chigwell lady, Anne Scott. Finding the rectory at Upminster to be dilapidated, he went to live at High House, opposite the churchyard. His work embraced not only theological subjects but prolific studies in the fields of natural history, mechanics and physical science. He conducted experiments on the speed of sound and other acoustical problems. Derham's remarkably wide range of interest extended also to the arts of medicine (which he practised upon his parishioners), horology and astronomy. The tower of St. Laurence's he used as an observatory. In 1702 he was elected a fellow of the Royal Society and was also appointed as chaplain to George II, later becoming a canon of Windsor. He died at High House in 1735. Derham thus has a notable place in the continuity of scientific work in Essex, which, following the decisive contribution of Faraday, was converted to practical purposes in our everyday lives by men like Crompton and Marconi.

A less reputable resident of Upminster was Alice Perrers, who lived at Gaynes Hall, a house that derived its name from the Engayne family, who acquired the manor in the thirteenth century. Alice Perrers, celebrated for her beauty rather than for her virtue, is believed to have descended from a Hertfordshire family of the same name, although this has never been fully established. Whatever her origins, she found her way into the service of Queen Philippa, married William de Windsor and later became the leman of Edward III. Like so many other royal " ladies " of her kind, she could not resist the temptation to use her influence at court improperly, and thereby attracted a great deal of public hostility. These matters are always exaggerated, but there is little doubt that she interfered in legal proceedings for the benefit of her friends, which was naturally resented. On the death of the king in 1377 she was forced to flee and her property was confiscated. Parliament, egged on by her powerful enemy John of Gaunt, demanded her trial and she was banished. Eventually she was allowed to return and contrived to regain some of her former influence. William of Wykeham, whom I have already introduced in Hornchurch, managed to enlist her aid in securing his pardon from the Crown. She died unlamented in 1400.

Although it is not as comprehensive as in Walthamstow the area surrounding the superb Norman parish church at Rainham is still recognizable as the centre of the original village. Despite the increasing tempo of modern development in the town it is still an entity, the church, the hall and the inn providing the essential nucleus. At first sight the impact that Rainham's " village " makes is somewhat drab. Its jewels are not flaunted but are unostentatiously withdrawn into a subdued and prosaic background. Their discovery is therefore all the more rewarding. Discreetly masked by a canopy of trees are the church and John Harle's lovely country house. Rainham Hall is complemented by the pleasing frontages of the Georgian homes in the Broadway. There are the vicarage, which was rebuilt in about 1710, and, also in the Georgian idiom, a house on which there are four fire-marks, which is unusual to say the least. The restrained, even unprepossessing, frontage of this late-eighteenth-century façade is relieved by a pretty little leaded fanlight, which is the only gesture to the decorative arts on this well-proportioned elevation. It is all too easy to skim through the outer fringes of Rainham along the old Southend road, or even to traverse the centre of this expanding town, without realizing that side by side stand one of the most remarkable churches and one of the most exquisite Georgian houses in Essex. I dare say that most of Rainham's visitors, and those who hurry through, are unaware of its architectural treasures, for the remainder of the town is largely featureless and offers no clue to the precious kernel to be found within.

If the old village centre is one feature of Rainham Thames-side is the other. Here is a world of its own, providing yet another illustration of the great range of scenery that is a characteristic of this large county. Along the Havering border, down at the river in the vicinity of Rainham will be encountered the brisk industrial and commercial activity which this artery of seaborne trade has generated around the inlets and along the shores on both the Essex and Kentish banks. Here the Ingrebourne joins London's great river at Rainham Creek, which was opened by John Harle, the builder of Rainham Hall, to facilitate the wharfing business that he turned to from the sea after his marriage to Mary Tibbington of Stepney. This venture stimulated the economy of the marshland village, which has ever since been oriented to the river economy. But the riverside at Rainham is not just the dreary and neglected tableau that one readily associates with wharfage. If one can turn away from the industrial debris there are broad and exciting vistas of the river and its craft. The Thames has imposed much of its character on this part of the borough. It has at once clamped the imprint of commerce and industry on the river line of Essex and added a further dimension to the local scenery. It refuses to be ignored. Across to the Kentish coast the skies soar upwards from the distant shoreline in everchanging patterns which on a fine day are reflected in the rippling surface of the tidal stream.

Another riparian community of no more than a few hundreds, though now expanding, dwells at Wennington among the pastures and gravel workings on the low-lying shelf that runs down to the river's edge. Here, focused on the thirteenth-century church of St. Mary and St. Peter, is still intact an essentially rural community with a place of its own in the story of Essex and of London. Wennington is associated with names famous in Essex history, like John de Vere, Earl of Oxford, and Sir William Ayloff, both of whom held the manor, but I would hold that its most illustrious resident was Henry Yevele, the great medieval architect. His name is perhaps the only one that in the context of English architecture can be elevated to the pinnacle of achievement along with that of Sir Christopher Wren. His unusual name has led to speculation about his origin that is still undetermined. It has been linked with Aveley in

Essex, which is adjacent to Wennington, but it seems more probable that he hailed from the Derbyshire village of Yeaveley. His association with Wennington derives from his ownership of an estate in the parish, a fact for which there is specific and interesting evidence. In 1391, with prominent local landowners, he was appointed to the Rainham commission of sewers, the function of which was to supervise the construction and maintenance of the retaining walls and sewers (channels) which formed the drainage system of the Thames-side marshes. In 1398 his name is noted, together with that of Stephen Lote, as a witness to a local deed. Lote, who also held land at Wennington, assisted Yevele in his work at Canterbury. Yevele was also a common councillor of the City of London, chief royal architect and, in a sense, an Essex commuter, for his presence was often required in London for one purpose or another and he would travel thence by boat, that being then more convenient than the overland routes. As an architect Yevele's was the great name of the Gothic tradition. His work exhibits a mastery of perspective, fenestration and design. It was in his work that the transition from Norman mass to Gothic line reached its purest expression. In Essex he was responsible for the Moulsham bridge at Chelmsford, but his greatest work was in the nave and west cloisters of Westminster Abbey and the superlative Westminster Hall, in which the great hammerbeam roof, the work of Hugh Herland, is perfectly balanced by the Gothic form and decoration of the building as a whole. The people of Wennington may thus look with a certain amount of domestic pride on the finest architecture in the capital, rivalled in my view only by St. Paul's.

Cranham, although now integrated with Upminster, is an ancient and separate parish of Saxon lineage. It also, by an historical coincidence, enjoys an association with the modern Anglo-Saxon migration that colonized the New World, for General James Oglethorpe, the founder of Georgia, lived and died at Cranham Hall. Oglethorpe was born in London in 1696 and went up to Corpus Christi at Oxford at the age of eighteen. His restless disposition took him to Europe and soldiering before completing his studies and he served as an aide-de-camp to Prince Eugène in the Turkish campaign of 1716-7. By 1722 he had returned to England and entered Parliament as the member for Haslemere in Surrey and distinguished himself by raising the then unfashionable subject of penal reform. At the time the English colonies in North America were under pressure from the Spanish in Florida and the French in Louisiana. Strategic considerations therefore prompted the settlement of a colony between Carolina and Florida, and Oglethorpe proposed that it should be established with indigent families of good character. Thus Georgia, the last of the original thirteen colonies which later formed the United States, was founded by Oglethorpe and named after George II, who sanctioned the project in 1732. Among those in the enterprise were John and Charles Wesley and parties of Protestants seeking the religious tolerance of a new and free society. Oglethorpe's administration of the new colony was marked by his successful relations with the indigenous Indians, the prohibition of rum and slavery and a spirited defence against Spanish incursion. In the later stages of his governorship he gradually lost public support, and this prompted his return to England. During the Scottish rebellion of 1745 he was court-martialled for alleged sympathy with the Scots, his family being curiously involved with Jacobite politics. He was, however, acquitted and did not retire from public life until 1765. He then settled at the home of his wife, Elizabeth Wright, of Cranham Hall, and here he spent the last twenty years of his life, dying of a fever in 1785. A plaque in the chancel of All Saints at Cranham commemorates his burial in the parish church.

Unlike Cranham, North Ockendon, another of the outlying parishes of Havering, has not yet been engulfed by the steadily encroaching frontiers of urban accretion in the Upminster area. It lies, still relatively undisturbed, in an agricultural landscape laced with pleasantly winding country lanes which only reluctantly admit their incorporation in the metropolitan area. The parish church has to be sought at the end of a shaded, tree-lined lane among the farms that still flourish in this rural corner of Havering. St. Mary Magdalene is a pleasing and interesting building best known among ecclesiologists for the Poyntz chapel, which contains as impressive an array of memorial tablets and sculptured figures commemorating that notable local family as would compare with any in Essex. One of its prominent members, Sir Gabriel Poyntz, was responsible for the presentation in 1582 of Robert Wilmot, who was a dramatist as well as rector. In 1568 Wilmot had the honour of seeing one of his plays being performed before Queen Elizabeth I. His play, *The Tragedie of Tancred and Gismund*, the plot of which derived from an earlier work of Giovanni Boccaccio, was dedicated to Lady Marie Peter and the Lady Annie Grey of Pyrgo in Havering. It was accompanied by some of his sonnets specially composed as a compliment to the " Queene's Maidens of Honor." In 1585 Wilmot was appointed to another south Essex parish, that of Horndon-on-the-Hill. He died in 1608. That this talented cleric should occupy a place in the literary circles of Essex in London is a consequence of the illogical inclusion, as it appears to me, of North Ockendon in the Greater London area, for it would seem to belong on geographical grounds alone to Essex rather than to Havering.

One of the treasures of St. Mary Magdalene at North Ockendon is a communion cup of 1561, and other churches at Havering also have outstanding examples of church plate. St. Andrew's at Hornchurch possesses a fine range of plate of the seventeenth and eighteenth centuries, which is noted by Nikolaus Pevsner for its artistic merit. It is well known, of course, that at the Reformation church furnishings, including plate, were destroyed on a vast scale and as a result there is precious little pre-Reformation plate remaining in our churches. In the whole of England there are only about fifty chalices and fewer than 100 patens. Subsequent to the Reformation, in the reign of Edward VI, the chalice was replaced by the communion cup. In Essex there are only half a dozen pre-Reformation pieces and none at all in the churches of Essex in London. The earliest example in this area is the cup of North Ockendon, although there are cups and patens of 1563 at Dagenham, East Ham, Rainham and Hornchurch. Many of the other churches of metropolitan Essex also possess plate of later periods, the only others worthy of special note being the silver-gilt set at Leyton of 1794 made by Edward Fennell and a Queen Anne set at Wanstead which was refashioned in 1790.

Havering is among the most fortunate of all the Greater London boroughs in the extent of its open spaces. Not only is it endowed with numerous parks, of which Bedford, Central, Dagnam, Harold

Lodge and Harold Wood parks are the most extensive, but it also enjoys a substantially rural environment. Along its northern and eastern borders a broad green crescent curves southwards from the gentle heights of Havering through Dagnam Park and Tyler's Common to the farms of North Ockendon and the lowland marshes down on Thames-side at Wennington. Only at the junction of Hornchurch and Upminster and at Rainham has any appreciable urban expansion as yet penetrated the green lanes and pastures beyond the Ingrebourne, which, though only a minor stream until it emerges as Rainham Creek into London's river, forms a natural boundary between metropolitan and rural Essex. The Ingrebourne, which rises near South Weald, is like another river of Essex in London, the Roding, an Essex river in its entirety. It is shared with no other county, unlike the boundary rivers, the Thames, the Lea and the Stour.

As we have seen, one of the characteristics of Havering is the continued survival of small independent communities like Rainham, North Ockendon, Wennington and, indeed, Havering itself, for in contrast with the other Greater London boroughs of Essex it is not essentially part of the continuous area of the capital's sprawling suburbs. It still has its own green barrier which at present continues to resist the demands of London's advancing limits. The main traffic artery in Havering is the Southend road, which strikes right across the borough, skirting Gidea Park, which lies south of its route, and the recently developed Harold Hill, which lies to the north. At the well-known Gallows Corner the old Roman road crosses the new road as it drives north-eastwards to Colchester and the east coast resorts. Numberless people traverse the borough on these routes, but they receive no more than a fleeting impression. Few will know whether they are in Essex or London, for the urban heart of the borough lies to the south of the trunk route. It is centred on Romford, where busy lateral routes through Havering meet just west of the market place, provoking the inevitable hurly-burly and cacophony of frustrated traffic. From here too the residential areas of the borough fan out in more or less concentric sweeps of terraced, semi-detached and more substantial dwellings. If there were not so many commuters it would be appropriate to refer to Havering's urban core as a satellite of the metropolis rather than a suburb, with its axis pivoted on Romford and Hornchurch. Havering's general character is indeed still that of a residential district, for although manufacturing and light industries have been established on an increasing scale since the mid-thirties, particularly to the west of the Ingrebourne, they have not yet made a substantial impact on the face of the area as a whole. However, industrial development is not all recent, for both Romford and Hornchurch were minor centres of industrial activity in the nineteenth century, breweries, tanneries and manufactories of agricultural equipment being the principal enterprises. Today the range of Havering's industries has extended to include light engineering, chemicals, plastics, textiles and other goods.

As development proceeds we may expect the face of Havering to change. The town centre at Romford is being redeveloped fundamentally, and throughout the area fine modern buildings, commercial, educational and domestic, are beginning to impart a new image to the borough. Somehow they seem here, in the context of Havering's more spacious quarters and rural perimeter, to be less incongruous than the glass-fretted elevations of the structures that now tower above the congested streets of Newham and the other Essex boroughs. The ancient liberty will bear its modern mantle well.

NEWHAM

London over the Lea

NOWHERE in metropolitan Essex has London so obviously devoured the Essex countryside as in Newham, which stretches down to Thames-side and is bordered east and west by the Roding and the Lea. Whereas in Havering the county and the capital are still contesting the character of the borough, in Newham Essex has retreated for ever. Here it was that London first made its claims on the green pastures beyond the Lea. The inevitability of the industrial and maritime development eastwards along London's river now seems obvious. Yet the capital was contained for centuries until its confrontation with the expanding population and the demands of the vast world-wide seaborne trade unleashed by the industrial revolution. From time immemorial Essex farmers had grazed their idling sheep and tilled their tranquil lands on the flat, grassy marshlands around the Hams. At the time of the Domesday survey two familiar figures in Norman Essex,

Robert Gernon and Ranulf Peverel, held the two manors in Hamme, which was otherwise essentially a single community living in scattered dwellings and numbering no more than about 400 people. Later there came the separate development of East Ham and West Ham. Finally they were united in 1965 as Newham.

As in Barking, the development of the locality was stimulated by the establishment of a monastic community. The abbey of Stratford Langthorne was founded in 1135 by Cistercian monks from Savigny and endowed by William de Monfichet, the lord of the manor of Hamme. Apart from their purely monastic activities the Cistercians were responsible for much of the agricultural development of the district and the reclamation of large areas of marshlands. Here also were established a wool trade and a bakery industry which supplied the capital. Rich and prosperous, the abbey held extensive lands in what is now metropolitan Essex, particularly in Ilford and Barking, as well as enjoying special rights in the Forest of Waltham. The Cistercians were dispossessed by Henry VIII at the dissolution, the abbey and its lands being surrendered by the abbot, William Huddlestone, in March 1538. The last relics of the great church were removed from the site near Bow Bridge on the banks of the Channelsea early in the nineteenth century. The area has now been completely industrialized, and it is hard to visualize its former splendour.

After the dissolution the area passed into lay hands, and so the manorial pattern unwound until the eighteenth century, by which time the suburban residences of wealthy city families began to modify the apparently changeless character of life in the Hams. By 1801 the population of the area had reached nearly 9,000, heralding the explosion that was imminent. Industry was already established in West Ham, in which it is still largely concentrated, East Ham being mainly a dormitory area. Calico printing was carried on in West Ham as early as 1676 and in 1748 the Bow pottery was established. Chemical manufacturing was developed at Plaistow from the late eighteenth century.

Throughout the Victorian century rapid and intensive development created serious problems of health and sanitation. Simultaneously with the growth of the industrial and residential areas, roads, railways and dock installations were developed. The West India dock on the west bank of the Lea was constructed in 1802. The port system to the east of the Lea was developed from 1855 onwards when the Royal Victoria dock was opened. The important road link with Barking was built by 1810. The Eastern Counties Railway reached the Hams in 1839 and the North Woolwich branch line, which traverses the abbey site, in 1847. The railway network was completed when the Hams were linked to the London, Tilbury and Southend line and the Tottenham and Forest Gate branch line.

In 1836 East Ham and West Ham, with Little Ilford, which now forms part of the new borough, were for local-government purposes a part of the West Ham union, which was responsible for poor relief and public health matters over a wide area, including parts of what are now Redbridge and Waltham Forest. A local board was established in West Ham in 1856 and in East Ham in 1879. West Ham was incorporated as a municipal borough in 1886 and achieved county borough status in 1889, a reflection of the extent and pace of urbanization in the town. East Ham followed West Ham to the summit of municipal status, becoming an urban district in 1894, a municipal borough in 1904 and a county borough in 1915. The population growth throughout this period was phenomenal. From less than 10,000 at the beginning of the century the population of the area which is now Newham was in 1900 about 360,000. A peak population in the seriously congested area was reached in 1923, when it was not far short of half a million. It declined thereafter as a result of the redevelopment of slum areas and the resettlement of working-class families at Becontree and other peripheral estates. It was a happy coincidence when, on April 1, 1965, on the fiftieth anniversary of East Ham's achievement of county borough status, the Greater London borough of Newham was formed by the amalgamation of the two county boroughs with a small area of Barking and North Woolwich. By then the industrial base had been widened to include engineering, chemicals, sugar refining, electrical products, confectionery, distilling and the Beckton gasworks, which was the largest in Europe. The former East Ham town hall, built with typical Victorian pomposity some seventy years ago in a Tudoresque baroque and taken over as the centre of local government in Newham, thus presided over a major urban and industrial community which had declined to 260,000 people as rapidly as it had grown. The East Ham borough motto, " Progress with the people," was also adopted, the Newham coat of arms appropriately symbolizing the shipping, commerce and industry which dominate the economy of the area.

Uninspiring as it is today, there is still something about Bow Bridge to kindle the imagination. It was here that one crossed from Middlesex into Essex, and its historical associations start with the Roman legions. The first bridge over what was then a treacherous ford was built in the twelfth century at the instance of Queen Matilda, the abbess of Barking, who persuaded King Henry I of its necessity. A second bridge, across the Channelsea, was joined to Bow Bridge by a causeway built to provide a safe passage across the marshes. So called from its shape, the old bridge eventually decayed and was demolished in 1835. The new bridge, of granite, was completed in 1839 by Sir John Rennie and lasted until 1905, when it was replaced by an iron structure. Close by the bridge is one of the most interesting industrial sites in the area, for it was there that the Bow china factory was established.

Except in its archæological periods ceramics is, on the whole, a neglected area of craft history, but I cannot omit reference to Newham's place in this sphere of man's creative endeavours. It was not until comparatively recent times that Chinese leadership in the field passed to Europe. By then, the seventeenth century, English potters producing hand-thrown articles were operating on a small-scale local basis. In the eighteenth century an industry centred on London foreshadowed the large-scale manufacture of china and earthenware which later developed in Staffordshire. The London potteries were at Chelsea, Limehouse, Kentish Town and Bow. The two most important, Chelsea and Bow, were working in soft paste porcelain, but from about 1760 Josiah Spode pioneered the production of bone china, which is now the staple medium of the industry. It was in March 1868 that the excavations of the foundations for Bell and Black's match factory on the Essex bank of the Lea at Stratford brought to light the site of the Bow china factory, which until then had not been precisely known. Further work on an adjacent site in 1921 resulted in the recovery of various relics of the kilns and moulds used at this famous pottery as well as fragments of decorated porcelain.

A patent for the manufacture of fine porcelain by a then novel process was taken out in 1744 by a glass merchant of Bow, Edward Heylyn, and Thomas Frye, an Irish painter and engraver of West Ham. Their new process involved the use of a bone-ash paste which improved the firing qualities of the china they were producing. It is not known exactly when the first Bow wares were produced, since the earliest piece of known date is of 1750. By 1755 the firm was producing some £18,000 worth of pottery a year. Much of this was inspired by Meissen and Chinese blue porcelain designs and the factory was indeed named New Canton. Bow china is not always easy to identify because of the great diversity of subject matter and the fact that other producers copied the process and the distinctive underglazes. The mark, when applied, consisted of an anchor and a dagger. Frye was assisted at the pottery by his wife and two daughters, all of whom were skilled porcelain painters. Although not in the highest flights of ceramics, Bow pottery is important for the contribution it made to the development of this art in England to the exquisite standards of the late eighteenth and early nineteenth centuries. Nevertheless many handsome pieces, especially in the range of enamelled porcelain and the " blue and white " ware, were produced at Stratford before Frye's retirement. After this was occasioned by ill health in 1759 the high quality of the earlier period was never recaptured and there was a deterioration in the designs and textures. The works were eventually sold and the plant was removed from Stratford to the Derby china works. The Bow pottery nevertheless has a secure place in the history of English ceramics and its products are much sought after by collectors.

At the other end of the industrial scale Bow Creek was the birthplace of some of the Navy's most famous ships. One, the battleship *Albion*, built there by the Thames Ironworks, Shipbuilding and Engineering Company, caused a disaster at its launching in June 1898 when a platform collapsed as the ship left the slipway. This mishap resulted in the deaths of a number of the spectators, who were drowned in the Lea. In 1911 *Thunderer*, a super dreadnought, was launched at Bow and served with the fleet until it was broken up in 1926. The most famous of the company's vessels was, however, the Navy's first ironclad, H.M.S. *Warrior*. This ship, commissioned to meet the challenge of Britain's continental rivals, was built at Bow Creek and launched in 1859. Of over 9,000 tons and carrying an armament of some forty guns, the ship was capable of fourteen knots. In constructing this vessel the company heralded a new era. It was, too, in the forefront of the social field, being among the first to introduce profit sharing and in encouraging the growth of trade unionism. The yard at Canning Town in West Ham was opened in 1842, but, unable to withstand the increasing competition from the shipyards in the north of England, the company was forced into liquidation in 1912. It nevertheless played a noteworthy part in the industrial history of metropolitan Essex. The old *Warrior* now lies neglected alongside the Pembroke Dock naval base in South Wales.

In my view one of the most picturesque buildings in Essex in London is the Spotted Dog at Upton Lane in West Ham, which is the oldest inn in the borough, dating from the sixteenth century. Partly weatherboarded, it has a modest old-world charm and its leafy setting affords some relief to its otherwise dreary environment. Its name is said to derive from the time when the master of the royal hounds in Henry VIII's day maintained the royal kennels in an adjacent property. Farther along Upton Lane there stood, until a short time ago, a house which Newham should have cherished but which, fallen into decay, was finally allowed to perish. This was Upton House, a stuccoed Georgian building of 1731, the birthplace of Lord Lister, the famous surgeon. It is a sad example of the loss of a building which, although not architecturally of particular merit, was of national interest and ought to have been preserved. The eminent surgeon, son of a Quaker wine merchant, was born in 1827. Few of the great men of the Victorian age made a contribution to mankind comparable with that of this Essex doctor who revolutionized surgical practice through the introduction of antiseptics and modern techniques. Before Lister's enunciation of the principle of antisepsis patients undergoing surgery faced the twin horrors of blood poisoning and hospital gangrene. His work is comparable in its importance with the discovery of penicillin and antibiotics in our time. Lister married in 1856 Agnes Syme, the daughter of one of the leading surgeons of the day, under whom he then worked. He died in 1912. It is to be hoped that Newham will find means of commemorating his name in a fitting and enduring form.

I have already extolled the Norman virtues of East Ham's parish church, on which the relentless attrition of time has had surprisingly

little effect, but the years have erased the memory of a strange and remarkable man who lies buried in an unknown grave in the overgrown churchyard of this fine parish church. A visitor to St. Mary Magdalene will be unaware, unless he knows his local history well, that Dr. William Stukeley the antiquary is buried there, for he was interred at his own wish without any monument. Stukeley was born in 1687, qualified as a doctor of medicine, became a fellow of the Royal Society and was the author of some extraordinary works. The enthusiasm of this versatile eccentric led to the establishment in 1718 of the Society of Antiquaries, of which he was secretary for nine years. He was particularly addicted to the ancient rites and was called the " arch druid of his age." In his garden at Grantham he built a druid temple. He also published a book on Stonehenge and kept minute records of his journeys in search of antiquarian knowledge. In 1747 he was appointed rector of St. George's, Queen's Square, in London, and died in 1765. Bishop Warburton of Gloucester described this odd but erudite man as a compound of " simplicity, drollery, absurdity, ingenuity, superstition and antiquarianism "—a not altogether ill-assorted range of attributes. He published numerous works on diverse subjects, medical, antiquarian, scientific and biographical studies falling from his fecund pen, but much of his antiquarian work was unreliable and even imaginary. Married twice, he had three daughters, one of whom married the then rector of Pitsea in Essex, Thomas Fairchild. How does one assess work of such varied quality at Stukeley's? Perhaps Gibbon answers this by, as he said, using Stukeley's material but rejecting his fanciful conjectures. We can but hope that this restless mind has been at rest now in its unknown grave for over two centuries.

Newham's other parish church, that of All Saints in West Ham, is less well known but is in fact one of the best surviving medieval churches in metropolitan Essex. As early as 1181 the church was presented to the great abbey of Stratford Langthorne by Gilbert de Monfichet, and it remained in the possession of the abbey until the dissolution of 1538. Architecturally it is of considerable and varied interest, containing a mixture of styles from its Norman foundation onwards. Built into the fabric are also the few remaining relics of the abbey. Situated in Church Street, its dominant feature is the fine

Perpendicular ragstone tower, which dates from the fourteenth century. The remainder of the church shows evidence of the periodic development of the structure, the neglect of the seventeenth and eighteenth centuries and the inevitable restoration by the Victorians. The original building was reconstructed, in the Early English style, at the beginning of the thirteenth century. In the nave may still be seen the blocked-up arched Norman windows of the clerestory. The chancel aisles, in attractive red Tudor brick, were constructed around 1500. The roof is mainly of the late fifteenth century. Among the interesting details is a very good brass of 1592 commemorating Thomas Staples and his four wives. The whole building was restored in 1844.

Alongside Lord Lister's one of the greatest names in Newham's story is that of Elizabeth Fry. This intrepid lady was born in May 1780 in Norwich, the third daughter of a wealthy banker and Quaker, John Gurney. She married Joseph Fry of East Ham in 1800, and in 1808 they moved to Plashet House, where she found the quiet of its rural atmosphere highly agreeable. Her philanthropic activities led to the opening of a girls' school and a dispensary for the sick. The most effective and dramatic work of her life was, however, in the field of penal reform. The famous visit that she paid to Newgate prison in 1813, when she moved purposefully and unafraid among the prisoners, is now legendary. She was one of those rare human beings who combine the ability to embrace basic truths with dynamic energy and high moral standards. Her work made a lasting impact on our social consciences and attitudes. In 1828 the fortunes of the family business suffered a serious setback and to Elizabeth's great distress, as she was deeply attached to Plashet House, the Frys were obliged to move into a humbler home. The new house, Upton Lane House, later called The Cedars, belonged to her brother Samuel, who lived close by at Ham House, the grounds of which now form West Ham Park. By then her tireless endeavours in the penal field had earned her an international reputation and she was visited at Upton Lane in 1842 by Frederick William IV of Prussia, who had told Queen Victoria, who arranged the visit, of his interest in Mrs. Fry's work. Her life drew to its close at Ramsgate shortly afterwards, in 1845.

Newham shares with two other Greater London boroughs in Essex the associations with one of Britain's naval heroes of World War I. John Cornwell was born on January 8, 1900, in Clyde Place, a withdrawn and humble corner of Leyton in Waltham Forest. He attended the local elementary school at Farmer Road, which is now a secondary modern school and renamed the George Mitchell school. Later he was at school in Manor Park. Having barely left his schooldays behind, Cornwell found himself as a boy first class in the Royal Navy on board H.M.S. *Chester* in the forefront of the battle of Jutland on May 31, 1916. The sixteen-year-old lad acquitted himself with exemplary bravery, staying at his gun position in the heavily damaged ship until the end of the action. The remainder of the gun's crew were killed and Cornwell received wounds from which he also died. The captain of H.M.S. *Chester* wrote to Jack Cornwell's mother: " I know you would want to know of the splendid courage and fortitude shown by your son during action. . . . The wounds which resulted in his death were received in the first few minutes. . . . He remained steady at his post. . . . He felt that he might be needed, and indeed he might have been; so he stayed there waiting under heavy fire and with only his brave heart and God's help to support him. I cannot express to you my admiration of the son you have lost from this world. I have not failed to bring his name prominently before my Admiral." In his dispatches after the battle Admiral Beatty commended Cornwell's courage and as a result he was posthumously awarded the Victoria Cross. The young hero was buried in the Manor Park cemetery, which is now in Newham. The fund established in his memory was used to maintain six cottages at Hornchurch for disabled seamen and their families. Cornwell's gallantry deserves to rank in the gallery of Essex heroes with that of the Saxon alderman Brihtnoth, who died at the hands of the Danes at Maldon, and the self-sacrifice of Captain Oates of Gestingthorpe, who perished in the Antarctic with Scott's expedition.

Many Essex men have devoted themselves to natural history, the most outstanding perhaps being John Ray, of Black Notley, whose biographer was William Derham, the rector of Upminster from 1689-1735, but the role of south-west Essex is not limited to that. The area can boast many naturalists whose scholarship has contributed in good measure to the sum of knowledge in this field. West Ham has been particularly prominent. One of its residents, Dr. George Edwards, of Plaistow, who was born at Stratford in 1693, was noted for his studies of fossils and for his great history of birds compiled over a period of twenty years. Librarian of the Royal College of Physicians and fellow of the Royal Society, this distinguished scientist produced a remarkable set of coloured drawings of birds, which is kept at the central library of the borough. West Ham Park was once developed as one of the finest botanical gardens in Europe by the Quaker physician Dr. John Fothergill. Here he specialized in the cultivation of rare plants. Later, Lord Lister's younger brother Arthur, also born at Upton House, established himself as a botanist with a reputation for his research on *Mycetozoa*. He died in 1908 and is buried at Leytonstone. Science has, of course, reached a level of sophistication undreamed of by these pioneers, but one is bound to admire the tenacity and integrity with which they pursued their studies. The traditions they established are reflected in the enthusiasm for natural history that is so evident in this area today.

Before leaving the subject of natural history I hope I may be permitted what some may regard as a minor digression, though it is to some extent germane to one aspect of life in eighteenth-century Newham. There cannot be many hedgehogs in Newham today, though they are not uncommon in the forest boroughs. Not infrequently one is saddened by the sight of one of these quaint but attractive little creatures lying crushed on the forest roads. The modern motor-car is now presumably the main enemy, and one against whom the urchin's spines are no protection. Today we are tolerant, even indulgent, of their irregular meanderings, but it was not always so. It is not generally known that, despite their usefulness in devouring insects of all kinds, hedgehogs were once regarded as vermin and there was a payment for their destruction. The vestry minutes and accounts for the West Ham parish in the eighteenth century, in common with many others, show that the price of fourpence, not then a trifling sum, was regularly paid for the capture of hedgehogs. The local farmers, who grazed their cattle on the reclaimed marshes lying in the south of the parish, believed the old superstition that hedgehogs destroy the teats of cows resting on the ground. Although regarded as insectivorous, hedgehogs are in fact omniverous and will certainly enjoy milk, but it is highly unlikely that they have ever been a danger to cows. The East Ham vestry was on stronger ground in encouraging the destruction of polecats, which then abounded in the district.

Although they arrive in considerable quantities in the docks at Newham we would today hardly associate table wines with Essex in London, but in fact good vintages were produced in the area in times past. A particularly bold, perhaps reckless, venture was launched at Plaistow by one Aaron Hill, who lived in a large old building called Hyde House. Before describing this somewhat feckless poet's grandiose schemes let us reflect briefly on English vineyards.

The Romans cultivated grapes in Sussex on the chalk of the lower slopes of the South Downs. Bede too makes reference to vineyards in eighth-century Saxon England, and some forty vineyards are recorded in the Domesday survey, mostly in Gloucestershire, Kent and East Anglia. A number of these were in Essex, for example at Stebbing, Great Waltham and Castle Hedingham. Usually the vineyards at that time were cultivated by monastic communities and the production of wine was for domestic consumption and was never developed to a commercial level. Grapes for wine were grown in the south of England on a fairly large scale from the seventeenth to the early nineteenth centuries. The Earl of Salisbury planted an extensive area of vines on the banks of the River Lea in Hertfordshire and Pepys, recording one of his visits to Walthamstow, praises the wine produced in the local vineyards. In his *Rural Rides* William Cobbett wrote, in 1823, of Selborne in Hampshire: " I have never seen such quantities of grapes upon any vines as I see upon the vines in this village." At Barking there were vineyards by the abbey, and early place-names, including Vineyard Lane and Vineyard Field, are indicative of well-established cultivation of grapes for wine. Although there has been some recent revival of viticulture in this country it had been virtually abandoned by the end of the nineteenth century and has never really recovered in the face of overseas competition.

Plaistow, I suppose, is a place that one retires from rather than to, but this was not always so, as I discovered from an anonymous poem in the *London Magazine* of 1734. In a rather jejune verse about the merits of Plaistow the relevant lines ran as follows:

> " You that a soft retirement chose
> May here enjoy a safe retreat.
> Here you are free from noise and strife
> And all those carking cares of life."

However, Aaron Hill followed this poetic advice, for in 1738 he settled at Plaistow, then a pleasant village, though, as he said, like most of the Thames-side parishes afflicted with " a moist, malignant air " which was regarded as most unhealthy by strangers. In Hill's defence it is only fair to add that there is nothing to suggest that the trite verse I have quoted is attributable to him. Of a Wiltshire family, he married a Stratford girl, who bore him nine children. Dramatist, traveller and minor poet, he died in 1749 and was buried in Westminster Abbey. Apart from his plantation at Plaistow his other claims to fame were a scheme to colonize Georgia and a patent for extracting oil from beechmast. Needless to say, he was also interested in schemes for the repair of the Dagenham breach. But none of his wild ideas ever bore fruit—almost literally in the case of his vines, the failure of which occasioned serious financial loss.

Despite the rapid depopulation of Newham in the twentieth century and the vigorous redevelopment that is now taking place the borough is still basically Victorian territory. It is from the proud queen's time that the housing, docks, railways and industry mainly date. Hers was the century in which Newham as we know it today was created. Although we may now encounter the towering twentieth-century homes of Newham's modern generation they are as yet but symbols of an unfulfilled future. Newham is still a fundamentally East End suburb. The former county boroughs of West Ham and East Ham were but the logical extensions of Stepney and Poplar. The humble nineteenth-century terraced dwellings in grey-black London stock on the tired and insalubrious acres of the erstwhile Thames-side pastures belong to the same pattern of life as the industrial and maritime installations that form an integral part of the London riverside complex from Wapping to Dagenham. There is no residential area in the borough in which at least some light industry does not co-exist with the homes of Newham's quarter of a million people. In area Newham roughly equates with Barking or Waltham Forest, but it is the most densely populated of the Essex boroughs. However, as a result of the decline in the population its density is by no means as high as that of Hackney or Islington and a number of the other Greater London boroughs, but the non-residential dockside and industrial areas distort this picture, tending statistically to minimize the congestion of Newham's streets, which is only marginally relieved by the relatively few minor parks and open spaces.

The generality of the topographical survey that I have so far ventured has thus a sombre image, and no one will pretend that Newham is an attractive suburb, yet it is in many respects lively and exciting. The masts and cranes of dockland litter the riverside horizons; along by Woolwich Reach and Gallions Reach is a romantic world of ships and industry. In a sense Newham's horizons, more than anywhere else in Essex in London, stretch far away across the seas to exotic and legendary places. Tramps from the Mediterranean, steamers from the Orient and the Antipodes and tankers from the Middle East kindle the imagination. Fussing, chugging tugs, the work-horses of London's river, and those docile beasts of burden the familiar Thames barges mother and service the great vessels that nose their purposeful ways into and out of the " Royal " group of docks. The perpetual seaborne traffic that throngs the river and the shoreside factories epitomize London's dynamic role in the economic life of the nation. It is to that sphere of our national life that Newham belongs. Of all the Essex boroughs Newham has the closest links with the capital, a geographical and sociological fact that distinguishes it from the others, even Barking. Its affinities are with Tower Hamlets, with which it shares a Thames frontage and a common boundary along the Lea, rather than with its Essex neighbours. It now belongs to Essex only in its historical aspects. Its topographical and sociological mores have irrevocably coalesced with the capital.

REDBRIDGE

Suburban Essex along the Roding

LYING astride the now diminished river which takes its name from the Saxon settlers who once lived in that exceedingly pleasant group of Essex villages north of Ongar are the former boroughs of Ilford and Wanstead and Woodford.

The River Roding is the physical axis of the new borough and, flowing on through Newham and Barking to the Thames, serves to emphasize the geographical identity of Redbridge with Essex and the other metropolitan boroughs. The name Redbridge itself was adopted from that of the old bridge which crossed the Roding at a point where it formed the boundary between the parishes of Barking, to which Ilford then belonged, and Wanstead. In earlier days the bridge was the cause of frequent parochial dispute, particularly over the responsibility for its repair. Now, appropriately, it is a symbol of the unity of the two former suburban municipalities of south-west Essex.

It is not known when the first modest wooden bridge was built across the Roding. Whenever it was it can safely be assumed that none of those earlier inhabitants of the riverside parishes could have foreseen that it was the forerunner of a not much more impressive structure which would confer its name upon the great modern borough of Redbridge. The first bridge on the site at the end of Red Bridge Lane known to local history was that which existed in 1592 and was then called Hockle's Bridge. By the eighteenth century it was known as Parson's Bridge, as it lay close by the reputed site of the old rectory at Wanstead. It had probably been rebuilt at some time late in the previous century in red brick, for in a map of the environs of London drawn in 1746 by Jean Rocque—which is, incidentally, a cartographical delight—it is marked for the first time as the Red Bridge, presumably in contrast with the White Bridge a little farther to the north. The latter, Woodford bridge, was a footbridge made of timber and, as with its predecessors, was often damaged by the flood waters of the Roding. Like the Red Bridge, it too contributed its full share to local controversy. In 1604 it was reported to be in " great decay " and its repair was the subject of frequent contention between the local justices and the lords of the manor. In 1768 it was described as " a founderous and ill built bridge " and it was accordingly reconstructed in 1771 in brick, with quoins and facings of Portland stone. The new and handsome triple-arched replacement lasted until 1962, when the present bridge was constructed. The Red Bridge, to which we must briefly return, was replaced by an iron bridge in 1914, but this in turn was demolished in 1923 to make way for the modern structure that carries Eastern Avenue across the Roding at this now historic site. As the river cleaves the borough from north to south so the arterial road, opened by the then Duke and Duchess of York in 1926, is now the logical east-west axis of Redbridge. Its construction led to the residential development on the farmlands which previously lay to the north of the route, thus serving to consolidate the whole of the Wanstead and Woodford area.

Before describing the modern developments which have culminated in the creation of Redbridge it is necessary, so as to assimilate the background of the borough's existence, to consider briefly the pattern of life in the area during the preceding centuries. In common with the other Greater London boroughs of Essex, Redbridge can look back to pre-Norman settlements on the lands on either side of the Roding from the flat pastures of Barking parish to the clearings that were made on the crest of the forest ridge to the north-west. Here was established an agricultural society which was not seriously disturbed until the nineteenth century. Throughout most of these earlier centuries Ilford was part of the ecclesiastical parish of Barking, and thus within the ambit of the great abbey's influence. Settlement at Woodford, beyond the Roding, tended to develop on the line of what came to be known as the upper road, which ran from Stratford via Buckhurst Hill and on to Loughton, although John Norden's map of 1594 shows only the lower road, which ran northwards along the west bank of the winding river over Woodford bridge and on to Chigwell. The main road system in Woodford— if it is permissible to term it so—of that period was completed by a connecting track following roughly the line of the present Snakes Lane. At Wanstead the pattern of settlement was based on the large estates, while the nucleus of modern Ilford was already apparent by the junction of the Roding and the old Roman road to Colchester, which coincided with the present High Road at Ilford. Little Ilford was just across the river to the south-west. Ilford village was linked to Barking, some two miles to the south, by a road running parallel to the Roding, which emptied into the Thames at Barking Creek. The roads of the district in the early seventeenth century left much to be desired and the lower road was often affected by the overflowing of the Roding in the winter months.

For the late eighteenth century we turn, inevitably and with profit, to the maps published in 1777 by Chapman and André. Based on a survey carried out from 1772-4, the scale and quality of these maps allowed of sufficient detail to record individual dwellings except those in towns and village centres, and they were the first printed maps to delineate minor roads in Essex. Woodford is seen to have been developing as a " country suburb " of London, with a strong concentration of larger residences along the upper road from the Wells to Snaresbrook. The Ilfords were still agricultural villages and Wanstead was dominated by the Tylney and Aldersbrook estates. These and the other private estates accounted for most of the property in Wanstead and there was hardly anyone who was not connected with the estates either by residence or by employment.

About this time the turnpikes were constructed, with the appointment of trustees responsible not only for the improvement and maintenance of the carriageway but for the repair of bridges and the management of the toll system by which their operations were financed. The term " turnpike " was coined from a military device used in the fourteenth century to obstruct passage on the roads. It consisted of pikes mounted on a frame and had a superficial resemblance to the timber pike rotating on a post by which access to the earlier turnpike roads was controlled before the introduction of gates. The transfer of responsibility for the roads from the justices of the peace to the boards of trustees was accomplished by piecemeal legislation but not without opposition. The farming community objected to the turnpikes on the grounds that it was unjust to impose an obligation to provide labour for the upkeep of the roads and at the same time to exact further payments through the tolls. These varied from a farthing for small animals such as pigs and sheep to as much as sixpence for a coach and horses. Under the Act of 1714 tolls could be commuted annually by monetary payments from the local landowners, and such appear in the records of the Epping and Ongar Highway Trust. Local resistance was in the end unsuccessful, which was just as well, for until the turnpikes were established no really adequate roads had been built in Britain since Roman times. It was the desire to construct a more direct route through the forest to Epping, and thus to avoid the residential areas at Snaresbrook and in Woodford village, that led to the project promoted by the Epping and Ongar Highway Trust, which had been set up in 1768. This was for the realignment of the trunk road from Epping to Bishop's Stortford. The work was entrusted to a famous road builder, John McAdam, surveyor to the trust, whose road through the forest to the Wake Arms was completed in 1834, thus shortening the journey to Epping by almost a mile. From the Wake Arms this sylvan route passes through several miles of beautiful and varied forest scenery and culminates in a stately mile of horse-chestnuts which march through Woodford with irresistible panache. At their most spectacular in the spring they would surely have delighted even Humphry Repton, who landscaped the gardens of Highams, which lies just off the road at Woodford Green discreetly screened by this leafy colonnade. The toll-house on the new road stood at the fork by Bancroft's school, but fell into disuse when the turnpike trusts were abolished towards the end of the nineteenth century. A secondary, but useful, connecting project of the same period was Whitehall Road, the construction of which was undertaken in 1832 to provide work for unemployed labourers.

With the advent of the turnpikes and later of the railways the growth of communications set the stage for the transition which was a common feature, as we have seen, of the development in the nineteenth century of all the metropolitan boroughs of Essex. By 1825 coach services were running regularly from Ilford Broadway and from Wanstead and Woodford to London. In 1839 the local section of the Eastern Counties Railway line from Shoreditch to Colchester, which was to become Ilford's commuter route, was opened with due ceremony. It finally reached Colchester in 1843. Originally of five-foot gauge, it had to be relaid to the new standard gauge of four feet eight inches in October 1844 to bring it into line with the rest of the system in Essex and East Anglia. By 1856 Snaresbrook and Woodford were on the rail route from Stratford to Loughton, and in 1862 the East Anglian amalgamation which formed the Great Eastern Railway led to further extensions of the Essex services, from which the future Redbridge boroughs naturally benefited. The Ilford—Woodford loop via Chigwell and Barkingside was added in 1903 and the L.N.E.R. took over in 1923. After the war came nationalization and the electrification of the Liverpool Street services.

Industry grew apace in Ilford, although it never developed to the same extent in Wanstead or Woodford. At the beginning of the nineteenth century a considerable brickmaking industry grew up along the Roding, which was deepened to facilitate the transport of the products of the brickfields to Barking Creek and the Thames. In earlier days the river, which rises some forty miles from the Thames near Great Dunmow, was navigable as far as Abridge, but when the needs of the building industries arose in the nineteenth century traffic had fallen to negligible levels. The brickfields on the Roding and along Ilford Lane heralded the establishment of the very considerable chemical, electronics, plastics and photographic industries of modern Ilford, which has a notable place in the industrial life of Greater London quite apart from its role as a dormitory suburb.

The fragmentation of the large estates in Ilford coincided with the growth of industry, population and local services. In 1830 the first step towards a separate existence was taken when Ilford was severed from the ecclesiastical parish of Barking. In 1854 a local board of health was established in Wanstead and in 1873 in Woodford. Ilford's final separation from Barking came in 1888 with its creation as a civil parish. In 1890 it became a local government district and an urban district in 1894, as did the neighbouring parishes of Woodford and Wanstead. By then the growth of Ilford was outstripping that of the future sister boroughs. The population of Ilford in 1901 was over 40,000. In Woodford the comparable figure was 13,000, in Wanstead only 9,000. The latter districts were united in 1934 and achieved borough status in 1937. Ilford had reached that landmark in its municipal history in 1926, but several subsequent applications for county borough status failed. By the time the boroughs were joined together with minor areas of Chigwell and Dagenham as Redbridge in 1965 Ilford's population was more than 180,000 as compared with the 60,000 or so people who lived in Wanstead and Woodford.

The relationship of the " great house " and the church is a familiar aspect of the story of most rural parishes, and nowhere is this better exemplified than at Wanstead. Here there was one of the most magnificent houses in the kingdom and there still remains the charming Georgian church, which, although humble by the architectural standards of its secular companion, is one of the delights of Wanstead. Let us first explore the part played by their predecessors in the life of the parish. The previous church, which was dedicated to St. Bride, dated from the thirteenth century and stood a few yards south of the site of St. Mary's. It was built mainly of red brick but the surface was stuccoed, and in the sixteenth century the church underwent enlargement and a square tower was added. Little is known of the early manor house beyond its name of Naked Hall Hawe. It was replaced in Tudor times by Lord Rich, who built a quadrangular mansion set in sumptuous parkland which abounded with splendid trees and shrubs. This house was famous for its associations with the Tudor queens. Here the Princess Mary spent part of her early life. She was again at Wanstead in 1553 when, on her way to London for her coronation, she was awaited at the house by her half-sister, the future Queen Elizabeth I. Elizabeth too knew the house well, and visited it several times as the guest of her favourite, Robert Dudley, the Earl of Leicester. During these visits she worshipped at the old church, and it is recorded that in 1578 a May Day masque by Sir Philip Sidney was performed in honour of the queen, who was said to have been much pleased. Not all her recollections of the great house humoured the moody monarch. It was at Wanstead that Leicester, to the queen's intense displeasure, recklessly and secretly married Lettice Knollys, the widow of Walter Devereux, the first Earl of Essex. To make matters worse, this slight to the queen was, with a malicious sense of timing, revealed to her by the French ambassador a year after the event.

Leicester did much to improve the property, but the burden of its upkeep was heavy and he died in debt, thus unknowingly setting an unhappy precedent. After passing through the hands of the Mildmays the house came into the possession of Sir Josiah Child. This able and industrious man started as a clerk in the East India Company's service, rose to be its director and made a vast fortune as a banker and goldsmith. In his diary John Evelyn notes on March 16, 1682: " I went to see Sir Josiah Child's prodigious cost in planting walnut trees about his seat, and making fishponds, many miles in circuit, in Epping Forest, in a barren spot, as often times these suddenly monied men for the most part seat themselves. He from a merchant's apprentice . . . being arrived to an estate ('tis said) of £200,000." Sir Josiah's son Richard climbed even higher in the social firmament. In 1718 he was created Viscount Castlemaine and, having demolished the old house and built the opulent Palladian mansion I have described in an earlier chapter, became

Baron Newton and Earl Tylney of Castlemaine in Ireland by 1731. The family's success and the splendour of their life at Wanstead endured for a while, but when, following the death of her only brother in 1794, Catherine Tylney Long inherited the estate Nemesis was at hand.

Meanwhile the old church had been demolished in 1790 following the consecration of St. Mary's, which had been built on land donated from the Wanstead estate by Catherine's father, Sir James Tylney Long. During her minority the great house was used by the Prince de Condé, Louis XVIII and the exiled Bourbons. On March 14, 1812, Catherine contracted what was to prove a disastrous marriage with the Duke of Wellington's profligate nephew William Pole-Wellesley. On marrying Catherine he adopted the family cognomens and became known as Pole-Tylney-Long-Wellesley, which name was naturally the subject of some contemporary humour. But the marriage itself was hardly a matter for mirth. The wedding was consecrated at St. James's, Piccadilly, by Dr. Samuel Glasse, the worthy and respected rector of Wanstead, its opulence and ostentation exhibiting the fullness of the family fortune which the wretched bridegroom was to dissipate in so short a time. His irresponsible and reckless conduct brought the property and its contents to the sale rooms by 1822. When in the summer of that year George Robbinns, auctioneer of Covent Garden, laid down his hammer after thirty-two days of the sale the contents had realized more than £40,000, which served to appease the creditors. No purchaser could be found for the house, which was taken down and sold for its materials in 1824. The unhappy Catherine died in 1826. The despicable Pole-Wellesley married and ruined another heiress, who ended her days as a pauper on parish relief.

Before leaving the subject of the church I must record the virtuosity of two other members of Wanstead's clergy. These were Dr. James Pound, who was rector from 1707 to 1724, and his nephew James Bradley, who served at Wanstead as curate. Pound, in the tradition of Essex clerics such as Derham, was a scientist, naturalist and astronomer as well as parson. His work on astronomy was particularly noteworthy and earned him the friendship of no less a figure than Sir Isaac Newton, who presented him with a telescope, then the largest in Europe, which had been acquired from Christian Huygens, the Dutch philosopher. The telescope was erected in Wanstead in 1718, but there are conflicting accounts as to whether it was sited in Wanstead Park or on the green. The park, which was then private land, would seem more likely. It was mounted on a pole 125 feet high which had once served as a maypole in the Strand and had been declined by Derham, to whom it had been offered for a similar purpose. From the evidence of Pound's account book in which he records the costs of its erection it appears that the largest item was the cost of drink for the thirsty labourers who raised it!

The rector died in November 1724 and was buried in the chancel of the old church at Wanstead. The pole, beyond repair, was dismantled in 1728, though some parts of the Huygens telescope are still retained by the Royal Society. Mrs. Pound went to live on her brother's estate in Wanstead, The Grove, and James Bradley sometimes lodged there when visiting the district. Bradley, who had assisted his uncle with astronomical research, earned distinction for the important contribution he made to the techniques and apparatus of astronomy. His most famous discovery, made in 1728, was the aberration of light. In 1747 he defined the nutation of the earth's axis. His scientific stature was acknowledged in 1742 when he succeeded Halley as Astronomer Royal at Greenwich.

Close by the Tylney mansion was Lake House, which served as a guest annex and was sited on an island in one of the ornamental lakes in the grounds. The frontage of the house was austere and undistinguished, but there was an imposing portico at the rear with a pedimented entrance and the dining hall contained a luxuriant Grinling Gibbons fireplace. Here from 1832-5 lived Tom Hood, who again recurs in these pages. At the house he wrote his only novel, *Tylney Hall*, but the damp situation undermined his health and shortly after the birth of his son Thomas at Lake House he left for the Continent. The child was so weakly when born that its life was thought to be in danger, and it was therefore hurriedly baptized at the house in a kitchen bowl. It is ironic that the gay poet's life in Wanstead should have been so burdensome and a pity that his island home should have been demolished in 1908. The present Lake Hall estate recalls this brief literary interlude in the story of Wanstead.

Also figuring in the Redbridge literary gallery are William Morris and Coventry Patmore. The Morris family came to live at Woodford Hall in 1840 when William was six and lived there for eight years before returning to Walthamstow. The house, a spacious Georgian mansion, stood in fifty acres of grounds bordering the forest just to the north of the parish church of St. Mary in the High Road. It was taken down about 1900. Morris's father was a wealthy man with a lucrative partnership in the City. After his death at Woodford in 1847 he was interred in St. Mary's churchyard, as also was the poet's mother many years later. Their imposing family tomb stands just inside the churchyard entrance. Patmore, who rejoiced in the forenames of Coventry Kersey Dighton, was born at Woodfood in July 1823. He at one time contemplated the Church, but turned to poetry at an early age, publishing his first work in 1844. In reduced economic circumstances he took up a post in the printed book department of the British Museum, and in 1847 he entered into a happy marriage with Emily Andrews, herself a minor author. Patmore's later work attracted the praise of major Victorian men of letters such as Ruskin and Carlyle, but he never achieved popular appeal. His death occurred at Lymington in 1896.

Hart's Hospital at the top of Snakes Lane in Woodford was the home of two of Woodford's most interesting personalities. This former Georgian country residence came into the ownership of the Onslow family as a result of the marriage of Susanna, the widow of the previous owner, Arnold Colwell, to the father of Sir Arthur Onslow, the celebrated Speaker of the House of Commons. This distinguished parliamentarian was born at Chelsea in 1691 and first entered the House of Commons in 1720, representing Guildford as a Whig. In 1727 he was returned for both Guildford and Surrey and chose to serve for the county constituency, which he represented until 1761. He was elected to the Speakership in several parliaments, the first occasion being in 1728. Onslow filled this office with great distinction and was much respected for his integrity and ability by the House over which he presided with dignity and authority. After his retirement from Parliament in 1761 as a consequence of failing health, he was honoured with the freedom of the City of London in recognition of his public services. He died in 1768.

Harts passed from the Onslows to a Cheapside draper, one Mr. Sherman, and from him to the Warners. Richard Warner, a naturalist, is notable for his production in 1771 of *Plantae Woodfordienses*, which although never published was distributed to his friends in scientific circles. He maintained a botanical garden at Harts in which indigenous and exotic plants were cultivated. There are interesting references to Warner in an account by a Swedish botanist, Pehr Kalm, of a visit he paid to England in 1748. During several visits to Woodford he was taken by Warner to see the Fairlop oak and was much impressed by the beauty of Epping Forest. He describes Warner as a well-travelled man with a deep insight into the sciences. In his garden, says Kalm, were " nearly all the trees and bushes that could endure the climate of England." Kalm's pages afford us, too, an authentic impression of the environment of Woodford. He writes of beautiful homes, fertile arable fields and verdant meadow. He notes also the excellent gardens and the great variety of hedging plants. The roads he describes as so full of travellers on foot and horseback, in wagons and in carts that one often had to " steer through them." Richard Warner, whose father, John, was a London banker, was born in 1713 and died in 1775. At his death his books and all his research notes passed to Wadham College, Oxford, of which he was a graduate.

We must now recross the Roding to devote a paragraph to Ilford's only surviving house of substance, Valentines, which is also of horticultural, or at least viticultural, interest. The old house was built in 1690 by James Chadwick and stands now with quiet dignity in the large and lovely Valentines Park, which contains some fine gardens particularly notable for a splendid array of rhododendrons and azaleas. Part of the estate was acquired by the Ilford council in 1898, when it was known as Central Park. In 1907 the house and much of the remainder of the estate were added and the present name was adopted. The house was famous for the great vine that was planted there in April 1758 by Sir Charles Raymond's head gardener. Of the Black Hamburg variety, it flourished, spreading some 200 feet along the south wall of the house from the vinery. It was reputed in its heyday to produce an annual crop of several hundredweight of grapes. Perhaps its most distinctive claim to fame was the striking of a cutting in 1769 from which the present famous vine at Hampton Court was cultivated. Cuttings were supplied also to other well-known houses, notably Cumberland Lodge in Windsor Great Park. But the old vine came to an untimely and inglorious end. About 1875 the new head gardener from Sandringham, " tidying up," decided to remove it. Just too late the estate steward arrived to see it disappearing in the flames of a bonfire on which garden rubbish was being burned. A charred fragment was salvaged from the ashes and affixed to the wall of the vinery. So perished the great vine of Valentines.

Ilford's other famous building is the " hospital," properly called the hospital and chapel of St. Mary and St. Thomas of Canterbury. By far the oldest surviving building in the town, it was founded in the twelfth century, during King Stephen's reign, by Adeliza, the abbess of Barking abbey, with which, as I have already mentioned, Ilford was then connected. Its original purpose was to provide sanctuary for lepers, which it did for over 200 years. The chapel, first dedicated to St. Mary, was endowed with lands and tithes in several of the neighbouring manors. It received its second dedication at the instance of the murdered Becket's sister after she had been created abbess of Barking by Henry II as an act of atonement. At the dissolution of the abbey in 1539 the chapel passed to the Crown and eventually it was granted to Thomas Fanshawe, who was required to provide a chaplain and maintain a number of indigent parishioners. The buildings were restored and enlarged in 1889 and the almshouses were rebuilt in 1927. Despite the tenor of life in modern Ilford the chapel remains a haven of relative tranquillity and charm, but its parochial duties were surrendered to the parish church of St. Mary when the latter was built in the High Road in 1831.

As may be expected, the borough enjoys its due place in the Pepysian annals. In August 1662 we find the Admiralty official in the Forest of Waltham to inspect the timber being hewn for the fleet. In the course of this visit he dined at Ilford, probably at the Angel, with a Mr. Deane, a naval officer, before proceeding via Ilford Lane to Barking, from where the timber was shipped to the naval yards on the Thames. In May 1665 he was at Wanstead, which he describes as " a fine seat, but an old-fashioned house." The next month he was again at Ilford with Vice-Admiral Sir John Minnes, awaiting the arrival of the Duke of York from Harwich. They were joined by Sir John Shaw and Mr. Neale " that married the rich widow Gold," but the Duke failed to appear and after eating " a dish of creame " they returned by coach to London. On May 1, 1667, weary and dusty after a spell in the park, he met Sir William Penn at St. James's. He seems to have had an arduous day one way and another, though it started well enough, for on his way to Westminster Pepys had met " many milkmaids with their garlands upon their pails " and " saw pretty Nelly [Gwynne] standing at her lodging's door in Drury Lane in her smock sleeves and bodice, looking upon one: she seemed a mighty pretty creature." The admiral wearied the diarist with an unlikely proposal that he intended to purchase Wanstead House, which would have been far beyond his means. Penn is mentioned frequently in the diary, though often in disparaging terms, so it would seem that Pepys did not regard him highly. But the Penn family is none the less to be counted among the most interesting of Wanstead's residents.

It is sometimes asserted that the Admiral's famous son William, the founder of Pennsylvania, was born in Wanstead at Sheridan House, but this can be confidently refuted. His birth took place at Tower Hill in 1644 and he died in July 1718 after an eventful life. The admiral brought his Dutch wife and family to live in Wanstead when William was very young and he was brought up in the puritan atmosphere of this part of Essex. These influences did much to mould his character and beliefs, and at Oxford he soon became involved in Quaker circles. Although they were reconciled shortly before the admiral's death, father and son were estranged as a consequence of the younger Penn's politico-religious activities, which landed him in prison.

William Penn entered American history as a result of the family's proprietary interests in New Jersey. The new colony was to have been named Sylvania, but the king, despite the wishes of the founder, who protested without avail, added Penn in honour of the admiral. William was appointed governor of Pennsylvania, but eventually returned to England for a period, during which he played a controversial part in public affairs. An entry for 1684 in the quarter sessions order book at Chichester in Sussex begins " William Penn being a factious and seditious person . . ." He was married in 1672 to Gulielma Springett at Rickmansworth. Unhappily and much to his distress, Gulielma preceded William to the grave, but he was married for the second time in 1696, this time to Hannah Callowhill of Bristol. There were three sons and four daughters of the first marriage and two daughters of the second. William's regard for Gulielma is evidenced by these extracts from a passage he wrote extolling her virtues: " She was a Publick, as well as a Private loss; for she was not only an excellent Wife and Mother, but an Entire and Constant Friend, of a more than Common Capacity and greater Modesty and Humility . . . an Example of Industry as well as of the other Vertues." Penn and both his wives were interred at the Quaker settlement at Jordans, near Chalfont St. Giles, in Buckinghamshire.

It is a pity that we cannot be certain of the whereabouts of the Penn residence in Wanstead where after the admiral's death in 1670 Lady Penn continued to live. There is some reason to think that it was at Sheridan House, but the evidence is inconclusive. That house stood between the George and Manor House, which survives along with a number of other architecturally interesting buildings in the High Street. Manor House is perhaps the most imposing of those that remain and the only one of its type in the locality. The sombre frontage of this solid house is relieved by the shell-hooded doorway, which, although executed by a rather heavy hand, is an engaging feature to which the eye is inevitably drawn.

No English village would be complete without its church or its inn, and each has played a part in the history of local administration as well as in the spiritual and social life of village communities. In the past several of the inns of Redbridge were, as elsewhere, used occasionally for business meetings of the vestry or of the courts. The Angel, which is the oldest licensed house in Ilford, served as the venue of the Becontree divisional sessions in the nineteenth century, being conveniently sited near the lock-up. The coat of arms of George I, which used to hang behind the justices during the court session, was removed from the old hostelry when it was demolished in 1897 and is now preserved at Redbridge town hall. Vestry meetings were recorded as having been held at the George in Woodford between 1694 and 1721. The White Hart at Woodford Bridge, one of the oldest inns in the district, was also used for this purpose.

In the eighteenth and early nineteenth centuries both figured in a more chacteristic role in dispensing their hospitality at the vestry dinners. These occasions usually followed the annual perambulation of parish bounds, which, by what would seem to have been an eminently sensible arrangement, generally started and finished at one of the local inns. The Castle at Woodford Green and the Horse and Well at Woodford Wells were also used as venues for these local gatherings, which suggests that the privilege, and the proceeds, were shared in turn among the local innkeepers.

The varied and fascinating names of inns are a relic of the Middle Ages, when the extent of illiteracy demanded the use of easily recognizable symbols for various purposes. Thus the insignia—no pun intended—of English hostelries tended to reflect local heraldic devices and personalities or to portray animals and other familiar subjects. The Spread Eagle at Snaresbrook was a good example of the typical coaching inn, and although not a scheduled call on the principal routes enjoyed the advantages of the local traffic from London to Woodford, Loughton and the other forest villages. The present building, known as the Eagle now, dates from the beginning of the eighteenth century. It was built in red brick and had a pedimented central doorway. A print of 1832 shows the inn with adjacent stabling and a blacksmith's forge. The building is now faced with stucco and Victorian reconstruction has considerably altered the front elevation, there now being twin bays and a pleasant wrought-iron balcony. But perhaps one of the best-known tales of Redbridge inns, which I cannot resist repeating although it is mentioned in virtually every topographical account of Wanstead, is of the cherry pie at the George, opposite the Green. In the eighteenth century it was known as the George and Dragon but was rebuilt and renamed the George hotel in 1902, when a stone commemorating the now famous episode was remounted in the south wall of the new premises. The inscription reads as follows:

" In Memory of
Ye Cherry Pey
As cost ½ a Guiney
That day we had good cheer
Hope to do so maney a Year
R.C.   1752 Dad Terry."

What actually gave rise to this touching but artless epitaph is not known, and various explanations have been offered by local pundits. The most likely seems to be that which attributes it to a case of theft, for a cherry pie worth half a guinea in 1752 would have been of more than ample proportions—and the amount of the fine suggests that David Terry was not unknown to the justices! Next to the George and Dragon were the village lock-up and Bodger's bakehouse, the perfect setting for the now legendary offence. The story is that a cherry pie had been sent from the rectory to Bodger's for baking and that it was stolen and consumed by a workman at the inn, presumably the unrepentent David Terry if the crude verse is to be taken at face value. He was, as the words imply, convicted and fined. At all events, and whatever the explanation, the story no doubt did its duty as popular bar-parlour gossip at the George and Dragon for many a day.

This example of minor crime was trivial compared with the more serious problem of smuggling, which was rife at the time in the Thames-side parishes. The lonely and secluded area of Aldersbrook was a natural centre for this illicit activity and provided hideouts for the smugglers, who stored the contraband in forest caches and other hiding places. There were constant battles of wits with customs officials and hard-pressed officers of the law in which all the traditional paraphernalia of this nefarious trade—fast horsemen, silent river craft and false-bottomed wagons—were employed. One notorious episode was reported in the press of 1773, when tobacco, spirits and other contraband goods were discovered hidden in an outhouse on the Aldersbrook manor, much to the consternation of the local squire, John Lethulier. During the same operation a number of smugglers' horses were seized in the stables of a gardener at Ilford. Such is the background of this now respectable estate.

One of the most enduring and creditable acts of the Victorian philanthropic movement was the establishment of the village homes for homeless and destitute children at Barkingside by Dr. Barnardo. A pioneer in this social field, Dr. Barnardo fed and sheltered the first of his needy children in a stable which was rented for a few shillings a week. These village homes should be a matter of pride in Redbridge, which did not always conceive of its duty to indigent children in such humane and altruistic terms. The Woodford vestry shared in the general enthusiasm of local authorities in the eighteenth century for transferring their human burdens elsewhere. Woodford workhouse children, like many from other local parishes, were " placed " under arrangements with the factory owners in cotton mills in the Midlands. In 1787 five boys and four girls, only eight to thirteen years old, were taken from Woodford to the mills at Nottingham, where they worked long hours and suffered harsh conditions of life. The parish records show that five more girls were sent in 1789. Other local children, with varying fortune no doubt, were apprenticed in London or other Essex parishes as another means of relieving the rates. The work of men like Dr. Barnardo thus brings us spiritually and morally to the twentieth century and modern Redbridge in its broadest concepts. His work embodied social attitudes and moral precepts which are today the bedrock of private and community endeavour. The social fabric of the great London boroughs such as Redbridge would be threadbare indeed without the weft and warp of human compassion and service that is epitomized at Barkingside.

The borough today is one of the most attractive in the London area. Punctuated by its village greens at Woodford, the Bridge and Wanstead, and lapped by the forest fringes from the Wells to Snaresbrook down to Wanstead Flats and north-eastwards to Aldborough and Hainault, it has retained much of its former rural complexion. In its residential quarters may be experienced the whole range of surburban permutations. To the north are tree-clad localities where blossom magnolia, laburnum and the other spring-flowering exotics that we associate with the homes of the well-to-do. In a southerly diminuendo the boroughscape shades into the more extensive semi-detached estates of the less affluent citizenry. In the southern districts are areas of terraced, square-patched-garden dwellings where the borough tends to merge with the topography of neighbouring Newham. All of these varied areas of Redbridge unite as authentic commuterland; its passport is the season ticket. But it is not merely a dormitory suburb, for it has an identity of its own. This is most apparent at odd and agreeable corners like Snaresbrook and at the green on the crest of Salway Hill. Snaresbrook has atmosphere. The elegant Eagle, the engagingly prim White Lodge, the dignified Royal Wanstead School and the familiar Eagle Pond in its forest setting all contrive to impose a special character on that part of the borough. The pleasant green with David McFall's splendid bronze statue of Sir Winston Churchill, which stands foursquare on Cornish granite at the commanding site at its southern tip, is a favourite venue. This ancient corner of Epping Forest, where the people of Woodford have congregated over the years, is overlooked by the superb Hurst House and the charming Highams and bordered by the glorious chestnut avenue. It epitomizes the centuries of local life that lie behind the Redbridge of today. Here and at that prosaic bend of the Southend arterial road where it crosses the Roding are the spiritual centres of the new borough.

WALTHAM FOREST

The forest borough by the Lea

THE landscape of Waltham Forest rises in distinct tiers from the winding banks of the Lea to the tree-clad horizons of the Epping Forest ridge. Between the extensive Lea valley complex of river, reservoirs and marshlands and the wooded fringes of the higher undulating lands in the north and east of the borough is the solid core of the residential and industrial areas. Except in Walthamstow at Church End and in isolated fragments of Chingford almost all traces of the farms and hamlets that characterized the area little more than a century ago have been obliterated by the metropolitan sprawl. Spacious days now departed are recalled in the substantial homes of the landed and commercial classes, a number of whose former residences have successfully resisted the relentless tide of urban expansion.

Until recent years the Lea and the forest had from the earliest times been the dominating factors governing the development of the area. Even now, despite the pressure of economic and social developments, they continue to exert a major influence on the life and character of the borough. It is not surprising, therefore, that these prominent geographical features, common to all three of the constituent boroughs of Waltham Forest, were reflected in many of the names suggested for the new Greater London borough. Thus Forest Lea, Lea Forest, Eppinglee and Waltham on the Lea were among numerous names for which claims to originality and suitability were advanced. Some of the names proposed were bizarre combinations of Leyton, Walthamstow and Chingford, but almost all contained one element or more allusive of the river or the forest. At one time it seemed likely that Walthamstow would be chosen, but the name finally adopted gave general satisfaction as being euphonious and appropriate.

The armorial bearings of the borough, as did those of its constituents, likewise accord heraldic prominence to the Lea and Epping Forest. A wavy line represents the river. A stag's head on a green background and a golden royal crown of the period when the forest came to be known as the Forest of Waltham symbolize the ancient royal chase. Three " couped " oaks acknowledge that Leyton, Walthamstow and Chingford are all forest parishes. Other heraldic devices are taken from the arms of important local families and institutions, including, appositely, the sword of the City of London. The motto " Fellowship is life " was inherited from the borough of Walthamstow and is derived from William Morris's *A Dream of John Ball*, an imaginary account of life in the time of the fiery Colchester priest who played a leading political role in the Peasants' Revolt of 1381. William Morris, about whom I shall have more to say, was one of Walthamstow's most eminent citizens.

This major London borough of almost a quarter of a million people has its roots in scattered settlements of the Anglo-Saxon era which date roughly from the middle of the seventh century. There is, it is true, evidence of Neolithic and Bronze Age occupation in the Lea valley, and at Leyton have been found, in the vicinity of Temple Mills and on the site of the Grange, relics of Roman origin which denote some minor settlement. But its recorded history really begins with the Saxon manors, by then largely in the hands of the Norman aristocracy, described in the Domesday survey of 1086, on which I have enlarged elsewhere in this book. The Domesday record, despite its functional brevity, illustrates clearly the agricultural background of these small rural communities, the total population of which, allowing for the uncertainties of interpretation, was probably around 1,000. The basic character of these small forest settlements was not decisively changed until the construction of the railway in the nineteenth century finally overcame the physical barriers to communications and development presented by the Leaside marshlands and the wooded slopes of the forest escarpment.

A railway reached Lea Bridge in 1840, but the Chingford line from Liverpool Street, which finally opened the way for the development of the area, was not constructed for another thirty years. The impact of the railways was dramatic. After centuries of rural life the Leaside parishes were transformed to surburban status in the course of a relatively brief but intensive period of residential and industrial expansion. Screened by the Lea and the marshlands, they had grown but slowly in the first years of the nineteenth century. The steep rises in the populations of the three parishes strikingly illustrate the fundamental changes that the improved communications precipitated. The respective populations of Leyton, Walthamstow and Chingford in 1800 were about 2,500, 3,000 and 600. By 1850 the populations of Leyton and Walthamstow were about 4,000 and 5,000 respectively, though there were still only about 900 people in Chingford, where the population had been static for at least two decades. But the arrival of the railway at Lea Bridge had in fact been a turning point, even though the actual spurt in population was delayed until the Chingford line was driven right through the area in 1870-3.

Work on the line began earlier, and by 1867 had reached St. James's Street. At this point the project ran into financial and other problems and work was not resumed until 1869. By 1873 the line had reached Chingford and was extended in the other direction in 1874, when Liverpool Street became the terminus. In Leyton a railway had by then linked the district with the east London network and extended outwards as far as Ongar. By 1900 the population of Leyton had reached 75,000 and that of Walthamstow 95,000. Chingford, still enjoying its relative seclusion, was inhabited by about 4,000 people. The two major boroughs were absorbing surplus population from the overcrowded capital and the agricultural economy of the area was yielding to commerce and industry. Various local factors retarded this process in Chingford, and it was not until the late 1920s, when there were still viable farms in the district, that light industry was developed on any scale. Even then it was confined to the area opened up by the new North Circular Road.

Although, therefore, industry made no significant impact on the area until the essential communications were established, the forerunners of the engineering and manufacturing trades of Waltham Forest had in fact appeared on the local scene at the end of the eighteenth century, when a plant at Temple Mills was producing lead sheet. In Walthamstow the British Copper Company, whose activities had been stimulated by the economic consequences of the Napoleonic wars, established a water-driven copper rolling mill by the Lea in 1808. The metal was smelted in South Wales and transported by sea to the Thames and thence by barge up the Lea to Walthamstow. The original building still exists, although it is now in the hands of the Metropolitan Water Board, the successors to the East London Waterworks Company, which had acquired the premises about 1860 shortly after the construction of the aqueduct which runs from the site to the filter beds at Lea Bridge. The building itself probably dates from the eighteenth century and, variously described in early references as corn mill, powder mill and oil mill, it occupies an important niche in the industrial archæology of Waltham Forest. On a minor scale, though not without interest, was the pin-making carried on at Hinks (now Inks) Green, Chingford, by J. S. Smith, who transferred the business from Southwark to Roper's Farm about 1850. The Chingford Historical Society possesses an interesting set of sample pins made in Chingford with the twisted wire heads which preceded the modern solid-headed pins. This small business did not survive long after the manufacture of pins was developed on a large scale in the Midlands.

It is both illuminating and entertaining to glance backwards in time through the medium of contemporary literature. This is a particularly apt approach to history in the case of Waltham Forest, which can claim intimate connections with such eminent literary personalities as William Morris, John Strype, Nicholas Breton, John Drinkwater and T. E. Lawrence. The River Lea, as is well known, attracted the piscatory interest of no less a figure than the congenial Izaak Walton. Long before his time the anonymous compilers of the *Anglo-Saxon Chronicle* recorded how in 896 the Danish force which had previously been ensconced on Mersea Island sailed their ships up the Lea, where they built a fort above London. King Alfred, who was endowed with the rare gift of both tactical insight and strategic grasp, at once exploited the situation. The river was blocked and drained, leaving the Danish stronghold isolated and untenable. The invaders were obliged to evacuate with the loss of their ships, which were destroyed or towed down river to London by the triumphant Saxons. It is not surprising that local traditions about King Alfred's connections with the area still linger in the legendary annals of Waltham Forest.

We may turn also to the intimate pages of the prince of diarists Samuel Pepys, and we shall not be disappointed. In his time two admirals, Sir William Penn and Sir William Batten, resided at Walthamstow. It was only to be expected therefore, in view of his acquaintance with these naval gentlemen, that the rising and ambitious Clerk of the Acts and future Secretary of the Admiralty should occasionally visit the Essex villages. We are thus regaled with amusing and informative glimpses of the local scene in the seventeenth century. In 1665 Pepys was entertained at Leyton by Sir William Hicks. He describes this worthy's house, in a characteristically frank passage, as " a good seat, with a fair grove of trees . . . but let run to ruine . . . and miserably looked after." The fare provided made a similarly unhappy impression on the diarist, for in Pepys's words Sir William gave his visitors the " meanest dinner of beef shoulder and umbles of venison," which Pepys scathingly asserts were in any case properly the perquisites of the forest keeper, from whom his host, who was ranger, had allegedly taken them. He was, however, well pleased by a Van Dyck portrait of Henrietta Maria, the queen mother. John Evelyn, the other great seventeenth-century diarist, seems to have fared better, for on May 23, 1659, he recorded a visit " to Rookwood [Ruckholt] and dined with Sir William Hicks, where was a great feast and much company. It is a melancholy old house, environed with trees and rooks."

On May 29, 1661, Pepys had spent the king's birthday at Walthamstow with Sir William Penn and after church enjoyed a walk in the " fine gardens." On the occasion of this visit Pepys participated in a race to Leyton with the two admirals in coach and chariot, which, according to his account, he won at the cost of spoiling his velvet coat, the roads being in a wretched condition. I doubt if the law would condone such reckless conduct today, but I dare say the coat would be safe—which shows how times have changed.

Daniel Defoe, whose journalistic genius and mastery of narrative have endowed us with a vivid, if fictitious, picture of life during the Great Plague of 1665, knew the district well. In his *Tour Through the Eastern Counties* of 1722 the same author notes the handsome large houses in Stratford and adjacent villages such as Low Leyton, Leytonstone and Walthamstow, and asserts that over 200 coaches were maintained in this part of Essex. The popularity of the Leaside villages as country retreats for the London merchant classes endured until well into the nineteenth century, and many of their fine homes still grace the borough today.

It was not only the affluent who made their homes in the area. Some very distinguished people in other spheres of life have dwelt in the rural environs of the capital. I have already referred to William Morris's early life in the forest. This versatile Victorian—artist, writer and the finest craftsman of his age—was born, the son of a city merchant, at Elm House in the spacious Walthamstow of 1834. His love of the beauty and solitude afforded by the forest and the west Essex countryside is reflected in the exquisite prose he lavished on the subject in later life. He rediscovered the peace and rural pleasures of his younger days at the mellow, grey-gabled Elizabethan manor house of Kelmscott, in Oxfordshire, to which he came in 1871 to establish his home and press. This sensitive and contemplative Victorian was the product of his social and natural environment. His artistic talents and versatility blossomed, under the stimulus of beautiful surroundings, into creative genius. He was inspired throughout his life by the Essex of his youth, and we can still see the fruits of this inspiration in wallpapers and furnishings that reproduce his designs. His work and influence are also still to be seen in numerous parish churches in southern England that were built or restored in the nineteenth century. Water House in Forest Road, Walthamstow, where the Morris family lived for a while, is now maintained as a centre of his work. In visiting this unusual but attractive moated Georgian house, with its twin bays and pleasant gardens, one is reminded of Morris's own views on fine old buildings: " They are not in any sense our own property, to do as we like with them. We are only trustees for those who come after us."

One of Walthamstow's pleasant and interesting old buildings, Walthamstow House, stands by the corner of Shernhall Street and Forest Road. This eighteenth-century brick residence, now St. Mary's convent, was closely associated with the Wigram family, who occupied it from 1782 until the middle of the nineteenth century. Robert Wigram came to Walthamstow in 1780 after leaving the service of the East India Company, in which he was a ship's surgeon. The iron cannon still outside the main gates is said to have come from an East Indiaman in which Wigram sailed. He entered business in the City and his success led to a barony in 1805 and his appointment as high sheriff and deputy lieutenant of Essex. After his death in 1830 the house was used as a school and orphanage before it was acquired by the Dominican Order. Since 1929 the convent has been in the hands of the Irish Sisters of Mercy. Entirely without ostentation, this serene and dignified residence serves yet to recall the quiet prosperity of the merchant class of Georgian Walthamstow. It was by no means the only large house in the parish to be used as a school. One, the Rev. Eliezer Cogan's academy for the sons of gentlemen at Essex House, Higham Hill, conferred on Walthamstow a notable distinction in that Benjamin Disraeli spent four years at this Unitarian minister's school, which existed from about 1800 to 1828.

Among Walthamstow's other prominent residents was Sir George Monoux, founder of the grammar school, Lord Mayor of London, mayor of Bristol and master of the Drapers' Company. To him is attributed the building in 1535 of the tower and north aisle of St. Mary's, the parish church, which is, appropriately, the focal point of the old village.

Walthamstow is a large and populous area, and the majority of its inhabitants are unaware of the " village " at Church End which has somehow survived the intensive development that has characterized the last century. Travellers through the town will bypass this attractive corner unless they consciously seek it out. Roughly occupying the probable site of the earliest Saxon settlement there are to be found, concentrated within a few historic acres, the medieval parish church and, circumjacent to it, a rewarding range of architecturally interesting secular buildings. The church is attractively sited in the green churchyard of the old village, but its appearance is somewhat spoilt by the cement facing which was first applied in the nineteenth century and has been renewed on various occasions since then. It is unfortunately necessary because of the condition of the brickwork it protects. Apart from the excellent

Monoux brass the church is notable for the monument to Sir Thomas Merry and his wife by Nicholas Stone, who was master mason to Charles I. Immediately to the north are the Monoux alms-houses, founded in 1527 by George Monoux on land formerly belonging to the priory of Holy Trinity. Part of the upper story was the original home of the grammar school, which remained in these premises until 1880. The almshouses, almost destroyed in 1940, were restored in 1955. This delightful red-brick terrace is balanced on the south side of the church by the fifteenth-century Ancient House and a small late-Georgian-type country villa. The picturesque Ancient House was originally an open hall building, the wings being added in the seventeenth and eighteenth centuries. It is now partly weatherboarded. The charming Vestry House is the best of the secular buildings and now houses an excellent local history museum, though since it was built in 1730 it has served as workhouse, police station, institute, private house and, as its name implies, the meeting place of the vestry. The house is flanked by a row of nineteenth-century cottages along Church Path, the main ensemble being completed by the Squires almshouses and one of the earliest national schools in Britain, which dates from 1819. The Squires almshouses were provided in 1795 by one Mary Squires for occupation by widows of Walthamstow tradesmen. Other build-ings of note in the vicinage are St. Mary's infants' school of 1828, the vicarage and the Connaught hospital of 1878, which includes the old town hall. Whenever I visit Walthamstow's village I inevitably find myself speculating about the odds against such a complete group of village buildings surviving in the heart of a modern borough and hoping that Waltham Forest will not allow it to decay.

One of Walthamstow's most learned and interesting inhabitants was Robert Ascham. He was born in 1515 at Kirby Wiske, near Northallerton in Yorkshire, the son of Lord Scrope's house steward. A highly intelligent lad, he went up to Cambridge in 1530 and his classical scholarship earned him a lectureship. In 1545 he presented a *Treatise on archery* to Henry Tudor at Greenwich, which so gratified the king that he granted Ascham an annuity. Ascham's intellectual talents received further recognition in 1548 when he was appointed to Princess Elizabeth as her tutor at Cheshunt, but after a quarrel with her steward he retired to the university. Later he was reconciled to the royal family and held the post of Latin secretary to Queen Mary, and after her accession in 1558 Elizabeth I appointed him as her own private tutor. Apart from his intellectual eminence he was a man of profound and humane instincts. His literary technique was interesting too, for he was one of the first authors to use dialogue to inculcate philosophical ideas. In a book called *The Scholemaster*, which he partly wrote while at Walthamstow, he advanced novel and practical methods for teaching the classical languages. Through the good offices of Sir William Petre, of Ingatestone Hall in Essex, Ascham was granted the lease of a farm at Walthamstow on the Salisbury Hall manor in 1553. He married Margaret Howe in 1554. After his death in 1568 he was interred in St. Sepulchre's, London, mourned by the queen and his academic colleagues, by whom he was held in great respect and affection.

Another of the borough's worthies was the lesser known Dr. Daniel Whistler, who was born in Walthamstow in 1619 and lived in what is now the High Street. Educated at Merton College, Oxford, and at Leyden in Holland, he became professor of geometry at Gresham College, Linacre reader at Oxford and ultimately president of the College of Physicians. Sadly, he does not appear to have acquitted himself well in this latter post, as he was reputedly negligent of its property. He did not, as is sometimes asserted, discover the disease of rickets or make any notable contribution to its treatment, but he was responsible for a valuable study of known information and experience greatly to the benefit of medical science in the seventeenth century. If not a distinguished president of the College of Physicians he must nevertheless have been a man of parts. Samuel Pepys, who occasionally dined with him in town and at Sir William Penn's house in Walthamstow, found him " good company and a very ingenious man." They also walked together through the ruins of the City of London to see the ravages of the great fire of 1666. Dr. Whistler is mentioned, too, by the other celebrated diarist, John Evelyn, and was a well-known figure in Stuart London. He died in 1684 and now lies in Christ Church in Newgate Street.

Among the great houses of metropolitan Essex was Forest House, which stood at Leyton in the grounds of Whipps Cross hospital. It was, sadly, demolished a few years ago and will be remembered for its modest urbanity and its associations with the Bosanquet family. The mansion was built in 1682 for Sir James Houblon, who, like so many of Leyton's past worthies, was a prominent banker. Its predecessor on the site was known as Goring House after Charles Goring, the Earl of Norwich, who owned it. Sir Gilbert Heathcote, an alderman of London and Lord Mayor in 1711, owned the house until it was bought by the Bosanquets in 1732. Mary Bosanquet (afterwards Fletcher), the famous Methodist and a follower of John Wesley, was born in Forest House in 1739, and it is her name that is usually associated with the house. The Bosanquet family continued in possession of the house until 1897, when the West Ham guardians purchased it as a home for old people. Architecturally it was not of outstanding merit, but it was a worthy representative of its age and in view of its Methodist connections its destruction meant that another valued link with the past was lost to the borough.

Another prominent personage to live in Leyton was Cardinal Wiseman, though he was born at Seville in Spain in 1802. He was at the centre of the great controversy over the " papal aggression " when, on the restoration of the Catholic hierarchy in England, he was elevated to the archbishopric of Westminster. A celebrated oriental scholar, he was the seventh English cardinal to be created since the Reformation. He also had a strong influence on the Oxford Movement and made a significant contribution to the theological questions of his age. His moderation and urbanity served eventually to subdue the flames of controversy which surrounded him for so long. He died in London and was buried at Kensal Green. His Leyton home, Etloe House, was built soon after 1760 by an eccentric scion of the Rowe family of Walthamstow, Edward Rowe Mores. This Gothic-fronted residence with its crenellated parapet stands today unobtrusively behind its brick walls in Church Road, where it serves as a nunnery.

★ ★ ★ ★

Leyton's parish church, St. Mary the Virgin, is comparatively modern, for no part of the present building is earlier than the seventeenth century, although the previous church was almost certainly on the same site. St. Mary's is an attractive building, trim and restrained, with a good brick-built tower dating from 1658 and surmounted by a pretty little cupola with a clock. The cupola was erected on the church tower in 1806, having been recovered from Sir Fisher Trench's great house, which was one of Leyton's most splendid establishments. This mansion stood in the High Road opposite the present county cricket ground. The clock on the cupola was made in 1768. Visitors to this church should not miss the Flaxman carving of the good Samaritan on the Bosanquet memorial, which will be found elevated on the west wall of the nave. One of the features of this church is in fact the wealth of interesting monuments, among them the commemorative slab of John Strype, who was Leyton's most eminent incumbent. Ecclesiastic, biographer and historian, this prolific writer was also the editor and enlarger of Stow's famous survey of London. Strype was of Huguenot descent, and although he was never inducted he was minister at Leyton from 1669 until his death at the great age of ninety-four. During his long incumbency he made, despite his expenditure of literary energy, a marked impact on the spiritual life of the parish. From 1689 to 1724 he also served as a lecturer at St. John's, Hackney, where he spent his advancing years in the care of Thomas Harris, a surgeon who was related to him by marriage. He died at Hackney in 1737 but was brought back to Leyton for burial.

Dominating the skyline of the forest ridge that stretches up from the lands of the ancient manor of Hecham, an Old English compound meaning " high home," is Highams. Now the Woodford high school for girls, this elegant building was the manor house of Higham Benstede, the name deriving from the de Benstede family, who held the manor during the fourteenth century. Now Highams Park, the story of the manor begins with the Domesday Book, in which a prosaic entry records what must have been a poignant situation when Haldan, a Saxon freeman, was dispossessed of his lands by Peter de Valognes, a nephew of William the Conqueror. From the playing fields at the rear, bordered with rhododendrons, may be seen, across the valley of the Ching, the manor house of the neighbouring manor of Chingford Earls. Brooding over the modern housing estate which has spread across the surrounding hillside, Friday Hill House now serves as a community centre. The present house, built by Vulliamy in a severe but agreeable Tudoresque idiom, dates from 1839. Its polystyled predecessor on the same site is said to have been destroyed by fire, but I know of no evidence for that view. It was the home of the Heathcote family until the death of Miss Louisa Heathcote in 1940.

The manor house of Chingford Earls was originally sited near
the Lea close by Chingford Hall, and it is not known precisely when
the move to Friday Hill took place. That it was some time in the
sixteenth century is clear, and it certainly preceded 1585, since we
learn from the Essex quarter sessions rolls of that year of a fracas
at " Frydayes Hyll Howse " involving the lord of the manor. In an
indictment of May 27 Robert Lee and a number of his tenants were
accused of unlawful assembly, malicious damage and an assault on
Henry Uvedall, forcing him to flee to Friday Hill House for the
" safety of his body and limbs." He is said to have despaired of his
life, and even when the door was closed on his assailants they
riotously " dyd besett on every side " the house into which they
tried to force an entrance, thereby terrifying the occupants. This,
regrettably, was not an isolated incident, for intermanorial dispute
was not uncommon in those robust Elizabethan days in Chingford.

It is impossible to contemplate the Chingford of Elizabeth's reign
without the celebrated hunting lodge coming to mind. It is an
essential part of the history of the forest and of Chingford. But in
the shadow of history is legend, and Waltham Forest, as a result of
its close associations with the Tudor and Stuart sovereigns, cherishes
its full share of attractive and plausible traditions. The best known
is perhaps the belief, no doubt embellished by time and telling,
which recalls Queen Elizabeth's visit to the hunting lodge, in particular the story of her mounting the great staircase on a white
horse in her elation at receiving the news of the victory over the
Spanish Armada. There are also the legends which attribute to
Stuart kings the ceremonial knighting of the sirloin of beef at Friday
Hill House and Pimp Hall.

An anonymous poet described the legend thus:

> " Quoth Charles: ' Odds fish! A noble dish,
>   And noble made by me.
>   By kingly right, I dub thee knight—
>   Sir Loin henceforth be.' "

In the popular version the story avers that Charles II, hunting
in the forest, was forced by a sudden snowstorm to seek shelter at
Chingford. He was, as was only to be expected, received with warm

hospitality, and in a high good humour he honoured the loin of beef with the royal accolade. There is some confusion in the various legends about the attribution and the scene of this royal frolic, and it must be admitted that there is no documentary evidence for it. In fact the origin of " sirloin " is etymological, the word deriving from the old French *sur-longe*, but it nevertheless seems clear that the form " sirloin " ultimately prevailed over " surloin " as a result of the prevalence of the legend, which certainly dates from at least the middle of the seventeenth century. It seems more than likely that the ceremony was enacted from time to time on convivial occasions in the forest area, though whether the monarch was ever involved is highly doubtful. Nevertheless, there was until recent years a Jacobean oak table at Friday Hill House which had a plate fastened to it claiming that the table was the original on which the knighting of the loin was first performed. At any rate, it is one of the traditional and pleasant legends of Epping Forest and deserves its place in any account of forest lore.

Another Chingford legend is that which tells of Henry VIII waiting impatiently at Pimp Hall for the sounds of gunfire from the Tower of London that would announce the decapitation of the luckless Anne Boleyn and forthwith embarking on a hunting foray in the forest he loved. In Leyton there is a tradition that Royal Lodge, which stood in the High Road at Leytonstone, was used by Queen Elizabeth and the Stuarts and that Charles II dallied there with the libidinous Miss Gwynne; but there is no foundation for this fantasy, although there was certainly a house on the site from the sixteenth century which may well have served as a hunting lodge. Royal Lodge was rebuilt in 1878 and demolished in 1929.

On a lesser plane there is a host of stories about Dick Turpin and his informant, the landlord, Dick Bayes, of the Green Man, Leytonstone. At one time Epping Forest was the haunt of lawless characters, and by the end of the eighteenth century matters had become so serious that nightly cavalry patrols had to be organized and an Act of Parliament was passed to deal with the situation. On one night Turpin raided Barking and Chingford churches, but he was frustrated by the prudence of the churchwardens, who had removed the church plate to their homes for safety. He eventually shot his accomplice, King, on Plaistow Heath, the culminating offence in a long series of squalid crimes. He paid the penalty for his sordid career at York in 1739. The notoriety of the locality for highway robbery is well illustrated by contemporary press reports. We read in 1750 that "yesterday morning, two young highwaymen, well mounted, were pursued, and one of them taken, near Chinkford in Essex," having just robbed a gentleman and his wife in a chaise in Epping Forest. It is also recorded that in 1757 the Norwich mail was taken at the High Stone. This curiosity, which can still be seen at Leytonstone, is itself a legend. The base is popularly accepted as a Roman milestone, and it is indeed probable that it was sited on what was a Roman road. It has also been suggested, with greater logic but less conviction, that it is merely an eighteenth-century folly.

An obelisk not altogether dissimilar in appearance to the High Stone may be seen near the summit of Pole Hill at Chingford, and many have wondered about its origin. One has heard wild speculation at times among visitors to the forest, but, unlike that at Leytonstone, there is no mystery about its purpose. It now stands neglected, its useful life past, for it was first erected in 1824 to serve as a sighting point for the Royal Observatory at Greenwich in fixing the northward transit of the Greenwich meridian, but in 1850, for technical reasons, the meridian was marginally adjusted and it now passes some nineteen feet to the east of the obelisk. In October 1884 the Greenwich meridian was accepted at the international conference in Washington as the zero of longitude and the standard base for time-reckoning throughout the world. At that time more than a dozen meridians served this purpose in limited areas and a number of others were considered, including ones based on the Holy City and the Great Pyramid. However, Greenwich enjoyed international favour and confidence and was adopted by a large majority. With the disappearance of the familiar expression G.M.T. from our vocabulary the significance of the forest relic on Pole Hill will recede even farther into the maw of history.

While still on the subject of these enigmatic symbols of the past let us consider for a moment those unobtrusive and simple iron posts in the forest at Snaresbrook which mark the old "Slype." The Walthamstow Slip was a curious anomaly of local government and consisted of a strip of land about 100 yards wide and three miles in length. It lay wholly within the boundary of the borough of Leyton, running from the Eagle Pond at Snaresbrook to the bank of the River Lea. Geographically therefore it had no contact with Walthamstow, of which it was nevertheless an integral part for local government and parish purposes. The inhabitants of the Slip paid their rates to Walthamstow and were liable to contribute to the repair of St. Mary's, the parish church of Walthamstow. Local historians have been unable to establish how or when the Slip became part of Walthamstow, although there is evidence of its being as early as 1677. There are traditional explanations to the effect that the land was granted to Walthamstow by royal decree for the performance of a civic duty, namely the burial of a corpse recovered from the Lea, on which the parish of Leyton had defaulted, but no solid evidence exists. In fact the existence of areas detached from the mother parish was not uncommon before the nineteenth century, and its origin probably lies in nothing more exciting than an inter-parish financial arrangement long ago. The first moves to abolish this particular anomaly were made when the Slip was included in the areas of the Leyton local board and urban sanitary district when they were established in the 1870s. Its final severance from Waltham-stow was effected by Order in Council in March 1885.

One of the best vantage points in Waltham Forest is Pole Hill. Its name is derived from Paul, and some local residents still call it " Pauli " Hill. This reflects the fact that this high land once formed part of the manor of Chingford St. Paul's, which was held by the dean and chapter of the cathedral, from which it was first granted during the reign of Edward the Confessor, until the Reformation. It is of interest that Lawrence of Arabia lived on the hill for a while, and the surviving fruit trees of his garden still linger on the west-ward slopes of the hill. Lawrence shared a bungalow with his friend Vyvyan Richards, a master at Bancroft's School. They at one time intended to print *The Seven Pillars of Wisdom* there, but the project fell through after the house was burned down. It was through Lawrence's generous co-operation with the local authority that the land was eventually acquired for public purposes and now forms part of Epping Forest. From the hill may also be viewed Chingford's present parish church, St. Peter and St. Paul, which was built in 1844 by Lewis Vulliamy and enlarged in 1903 by Sir Reginald Blom-field. The church is well sited on the old village green, having been erected at the expense of the rector, the Rev. Robert Boothby Heathcote, who was also the lord of the manor of Chingford Earls, as a replacement for the lovely old church on the Mount, which then resumed its former dedication of All Saints.

We have dwelt on the agreeable if nebulous sphere of legendary tradition in the borough, but from Chingford Mount or Pole Hill may be experienced the tangible prospect of Waltham Forest as it is today. This is the reality: acres of plebeian rooftops, factory chimneys and church spires, the whole encompassed by the wooded gradients and green contours of the forest and to the west the riverine landscape of the Lea valley. With the forest it forms part of the lengthy semi-rural circumference of the borough, which for only a very short distance along its southern borders is confronted by bricks and mortar. Travellers on the Chingford—Liverpool Street line will be familiar with the vast rectangular pattern of filter beds in the Lea valley, where there was not so long ago a picturesque reservoir studded with small green islands. This major new installation is the latest phase of the development of London's water supply in this part of the Lea valley. The twelve-mile-long network of reservoirs dates from the middle of the nineteenth century, when the development of public utilities was promoted in order to deal with the appalling situation revealed by various commissions of inquiry. The first installation, including the aqueduct, was in operation by 1854. The first three of the main reservoirs were completed in 1863; two others were brought into use in 1866 and the Maynard reservoir was opened in 1870; five more were added between that date and the Lockwood and Banbury reservoirs in 1901; the King George V reservoir at Chingford was opened by the king in 1913; and the last of the major reservoirs, the Girling, came into use in 1951. The Lea valley has thus been transformed and an effective barrier created which has stemmed the urban sprawl that otherwise would have engulfed the Essex bank as it did the Middlesex side of the river.

The river was the route by which man first made his way into the area, and likewise the valley has always been a regular migration route for a great variety of bird life. The huge reservoirs extend over much of the several miles of marshlands in the valley, which is a natural and permanent sanctuary. Ducks of all kinds, water birds and waders frequent the area; the migrants include peregrines, storks, buzzards, coots and cormorants; among the regulars will be found plovers, terns, redwings, wagtails, swifts, robins, finches and other welcome visitors to the gardens of Waltham Forest; there is also in the valley, on an island in one of the reservoirs, one of the largest heronries in south-east England.

The semi-natural environment of Epping Forest and the water habitats of the Lea valley have provided conditions which have considerably enriched the avifauna of the London area. Whereas atmospheric pollution and other factors have tended to diminish the number of breeding species in the suburban boroughs, conditions in the valley have encouraged its colonization by numerous interesting birds. Apart from the herons which have nested since 1914 there may be seen many aquatic birds, including the great crested grebe and occasionally the Slavonian grebe. Gulls, too, are common, and the evening migration of these scavenging birds, among them common, herring and black-headed gulls, as they return to their roosts in the Lea valley is an exhilarating spectacle. The natural history of Waltham Forest must surely rival that of any comparable urban area in Britian. It is a haven for wild life and human recreation.

Until fairly recent times the Leaside marshes were subject to Lammas rights and are still known locally as the Lammas lands. Lammas Day, celebrated on August 1, used to be of some local significance and many parishes still bear place-name relics of this ancient festival. The name of the festival comes from the Old English *hlaf maesse*, meaning " loaf mass," and parishioners would present to the church, as part of the custom of " first fruits," a loaf made from the newly harvested crops. The Lammas tradition dates from at least the seventh century. Such lands were normally enclosed by the landowners until the summer cropping was over, but the enclosure period was subject to some local variation. Usually the grain lands were opened on August 1 and the grasslands on old Midsummer Day, July 5, until the following Lady Day. In some parishes, Walthamstow for example, the period ran from old Lammas Day, August 13, to old Lady Day, April 6. The removal of the fences after the summer cropping, to allow pasturage on the Lammas lands for those with common rights, was often accompanied by some ceremony or contrived display of local enthusiasm. The grazing was permitted at a nominal charge of a few pence a head, payable to a manorial official called the hayward. In Leyton the Lammas rights were extinguished in 1904, the lands being safeguarded by legislation for use as open spaces or recreation grounds for the enjoyment of the public, but this was only after much public protest and some disorder. On Lammas Day 1892 a large gathering of parishioners pulled down the fences and tore up the railway lines which had been built on the Lammas lands. This spirited assertion of ancient rights led to legal action, but there was eventually a compromise under which the public retained certain open spaces, statutorily protected, and the public utilities the land areas essential to their operations. Although there has subsequently been pressure from time to time for the abolition of these residual public rights this has been successfully resisted. The acquisition of Lammas land for the construction of the railways and the waterworks involved the legal extinguishment of the Lammas rights. Those on the marshlands in Walthamstow were extinguished only after a prolonged and costly procedure under the Walthamstow Corporation Act of 1934. The settlement by arbitration of private claims for compensation alone cost upwards of £60,000.

Aside from these episodes of civic dispute the marshes of the Lea valley were the scene of an historic event in 1909. This was the first powered flight in Britain in an all-British aeroplane. The first powered flight was made by the Wright brothers in the United States in December 1903. Another American, S. F. Cody, made the first flight in Britain in 1908. Walthamstow marshes entered the annals of British aviation when A. V. Roe established his workshops in an arch of the viaduct on which the Chingford line traverses the marshes and the River Lea. On July 13, 1909, Roe made a flight of 100 feet over the marshes, landing at the edge of the river. On July 22 he flew 900 feet across the marshes in his 9h.p. triplane. Bleriot flew the English Channel two days later.

What of the river itself? The Lea certainly has a place in the history of Essex and its waters have been of economic value too, as a canal and as a source of food for the riverside dwellers of earlier times. Fish was in fact an important element in the diet of medieval England, and apart from river supplies fishponds were maintained to supplement other food supplies, especially in the monastic establishments. The Domesday survey of 1086 records a total of twenty-eight fisheries on the Essex manors. As would be expected, many of these were grouped along the estuaries of the Thames and the Blackwater, but there were a number along the Lea as well. The river has also been highly favoured among the fishing fraternity, as readers of Izaak Walton will know, and a great variety of edible fish used to inhabit its waters. Until the early part of the nineteenth century salmon were regularly taken from the river, but for various reasons these days are gone. Nevertheless, the Lea and the other rivers of south-west Essex continue to attract fishermen in goodly numbers.

In none of the metropolitan boroughs of Essex is the duality of its existence more apparent than in Waltham Forest. It is manifestly a part, albeit peripheral, of the great conurbation of London, yet it is divided from the capital by the waterscapes of the Lea valley and united to Essex by the forest. In its development to maturity as a borough in its own right, Waltham Forest, as Essex in London as a whole, may rely on the cultural and social lineage of both.

Queen Elizabeth's Hunting Lodge, Chingford, 1966

REFERENCE NOTE

THIS book naturally relies on numerous secondary and original sources which it would be impracticable to detail in full. The most valuable of these is the *Victoria County History of Essex*, and readers wishing to enlarge their knowledge of county history should refer first to this basic work. The *V.C.H.* bibliography volume is comprehensive and should also be consulted, but the sources I have listed below will be found useful by students and the general reader alike.

GENERAL

The Victoria County History of Essex	
History of Essex (1958)	A. C. Edwards
The Place-names of Essex (1935)	P. H. Reaney
The Buildings of Essex (1965)	Nikolaus Pevsner
The Dictionary of National Biography	
Essex Countryside	
Essex Journal	
Essex Naturalist	
Essex Review	
Publications of the Essex Record Office	

EPPING FOREST

Treatise of the Forest Laws (Fourth edition, 1717)	John Manwood
The Forest of Essex (1887)	W. R. Fisher
Commons, Forests and Footpaths (1910) ..	Lord Eversley
Royal Forests of England (1905)	J. C. Cox
English Deer Parks (1867)	E. Shirley
Epping Forest; its Literary and Historical Associations (1945)	W. Addison
London's Epping Forest (1950)	J. A. Brimble
Queen Elizabeth's Hunting Lodge (1965) ..	K. J. Neale

BARKING

History of Barking (1936)	J. E. A. Oxley
History of Barking Abbey (1954)	E. A. Loftus and H. F. Chettle
The Book of Dagenham (1937)	J. G. O'Leary

HAVERING

Memories of Old Romford (1880)	G. Terry
History and Topography of Upminster (1879) ..	T. L. Wilson
Ye Olde Village of Hornchurch (1917) ..	C. T. Perfect
History of the Parish of Havering-atte-Bower (1925)	H. A. Smith
A History of Rainham (1966)	F. Lewis

NEWHAM

History of East Ham (1922)	A. Stokes
Fifty Years a Borough; the Story of West Ham (1936)	D. McDougall

REDBRIDGE

Ilford Past and Present (1901)	G. Tasker
Wanstead through the Ages (1946)	W. V. Phillips
The Story of Wanstead and Woodford (1962) ..	J. Elsden Tuffs
Woodford (Essex) 1600-1836 (1950)	E. J. Erith
Publications of the Woodford and District Historical Society	

WALTHAM FOREST

The Story of Walthamstow (1952)	G. E. Roebuck
A History of Leyton (1894)	J. Kennedy
Chingford in History (1967)	K. J. Neale
Publications of the Chingford Historical Society	
Publications of the Walthamstow Antiquarian Society	

MISCELLANEOUS

English Windmills in Buckinghamshire, Essex, Hertfordshire, Middlesex and London (1932)	D. Smith
Windmills in England (1948)	R. Wailes
Pigeon Cotes and Dove Houses of Essex (1931)	D. Smith
A Book of Dovecotes (1920)	A. O. Cooke
British Fire-marks from 1680 (1911)	G. A. Fothergill
Fire Marks and Insurance Office Fire Brigades (1927)	B. Williams
Essex Blood and Thunder (1967)	G. Caunt
Notes and Queries (1859-1947)—*passim*	

The Eagle, Snaresbrook

INDEX

The classical doorway to Rainham Hall